D0868449

QUESTION EVERYTHING

ADVICE FOR STUDENTS AND GRADUATES

KENNY GLENN

Copyright © 2022 by Kenny Glenn.

All rights reserved. No part of this publication may be repro-
duced, distributed, or transmitted in any form or by any means,
including photocopying, recording, or other electronic or
mechanical methods, without the prior written permission of the
publisher, except in the case of brief quotations embodied in
critical reviews and certain other noncommercial uses permitted
by copyright law. For permissions, or further information contact
the author at:

info@kgmaximo.com

Ordering Information:
Quantity sales. Special discounts are available on quantity
purchases by corporations, associations, and others. For details,
contact the email address above.

Printed in the United States of America
Published by CM Book Publishing

First printing, 2022

ISBN: 978-0-578-28831-4 soft cover
ISBN: 978-0-578-29574-9 hard cover

Dedication

This book is dedicated to the student who lives within each of us. Let us remain inquisitive by questioning all things, thoughts, traditions, ideas, habits, patterns, systems, and rules.

As we graduate to new levels of life, we must continue to challenge any self-imposed or societal limitations.

Table of Contents

Table of Contents

Preface

I am grateful for everything that has occurred in my life! This includes the ups, the downs, the highs, the lows, the yeses, the noes, the good, the bad, the successes, the failures, and the seemingly random occurrences that perfectly aligned for the better. The universal law of polarity is a blessing, and I do not believe in coincidences. Instead, I believe everything happens for a reason and exactly when it is meant to occur. God certainly has been, is, and will be with and within me every step of the way. For that, I am eternally thankful. In the years before my 25th birthday, which is the day of this book's release, I have succeeded in several areas while receiving numerous accolades. Yet, I would not be as appreciative without the lessons I learned from trying and failing.

This book is based on my opinions and the lessons I learned from life experiences as a student and a graduate. I wrote this book specifically for students and graduates because I understand their pain points, struggles, and perceived limitations. It is not a direct step-by-step guide or a how-to manual, as I know everyone's path is unique. Rather, it is filled with the honest advice I would tell my younger self. Hence, you may use the advice where you deem it to be beneficial for you. As the author, I am simply offering an additional point of view. With confidence, I know that this book will impact millions. At least one student will resonate with it. That student will change their mind, which will change their world, and then they will create an entire lineage.

Note of Wisdom: Your parents, teachers, friends, family, church pastor, neighbors, people on television and social media, and even the author of this book do not have all the answers. They are just some of the resources you have the choice of using to help you find any answer that you seek. Everything comes down to a choice! Will you choose to find the solutions to your problems or choose to make excuses and blame others? You have the power to do and be whatever you set your mind to while living a life of abundance! Bob Proctor said it best: "If you can see it in your mind, you can hold it in your hand."

I exist to help students and graduates attain **freedom, independence, success, and health (FISH).** According to ancient Chinese philosopher Lao Tzu, "If you give a man a fish, you feed him for a day. If you teach a man to fish, you feed him for a lifetime."

Acknowledgments

I offer major thanks to every person who has had an impact on how I view the world and carry myself. This includes relatives who know me as Jamall, as well as, friends, classmates, teammates, trainers, coaches, and community members, who know me as Kenny. Of course, I must include the names of those closest to me: my parents, Kenneth Jerome Glenn and Glenda Maximo-Glenn; and my sister, Nahja Glenn. I thank each of you for the constant giving of love & support throughout every stage of my life.

I also want to thank specific families: the Abrams, Harris, Banks, Crawford, Glenn, Bennett, Martin, Kline, Johnson, Maximo, Oliva, Barcelona, Russell, Bunch, Gray, DeWindt, and Steele families.

People who helped me in this book-writing process include: Roderick Mills Jr, Ryan Billian, Benjamin Phillips III, Dr. J.C. Baker, Jon Ross, Derek Williams, Ali Barnes, Carlton Collins, Ash Cash, Sumair Bhasin, and my editor, Dr. Dabian Witherspoon.

SECTION 1:

THE FOUNDATION

You are always with your younger self

— JON SAXX

CHAPTER 1

Who, What, and Why?

Who Is This Book For?

This book is for the younger version of me: the student who is still in school or has recently graduated from high school, trade school, college, or even an online course; the student who seems lost and is just trying to figure out life; the graduate who is being pulled in so many directions and does not know which way to turn; the student who wants to fit in socially but also stand out among their peers; the graduate who has experienced trauma, even if they may not currently define it as trauma because friends, family, and mainstream media have normalized it; or the student who has an idea of where they are going but would not reject a wise guide who is willing to help them gain new perspectives and avoid pitfalls.

When I speak to students at high schools and colleges, it is like looking in the mirror at my younger self. When I was in their position, I experienced the same things they eat, watch, think, learn, and wear. This truth allows me to realize the struggles that students go through. While having numerous intimate conversations with peers who have graduated, I realized their similarities.

1

Even after graduating, most are still seeking their purpose and ways to efficiently achieve their deepest desires. The combination of my youthfulness and vulnerability, helps both groups relate to me and view me as a mentor. When people hear my age and story, they wonder, "How have you done so much in so little time?" As I offer advice, I do not speak to them as a demeaning, authoritative figure. Instead, I aim to inspire them. I want to truly hear and see people for who they are while helping them find solutions.

Who Is the Author?

On the surface, I am a son, a brother, a friend, a mentor, a Black American, and a Honduran man with Garifuna roots. My achievements as a student are noteworthy. In high school at Mt. Healthy in Cincinnati, Ohio, I graduated at the age of 16 as the top-ranked Black male in my class, my classmates voted me as "Most Athletic," I earned the "Conference Athlete of the Year" award, and I achieved the status of All-State in track & field. At Miami University in Ohio, I simultaneously earned my bachelor's and master's degrees in accounting, and I competed as a track athlete while becoming a three-time NCAA National First Round Qualifier and the owner of multiple school records. Then, as a college graduate, I became an entrepreneur, an international consultant, and a school board member. Next, as a Honduran professional athlete, I became a Central American champion, a national record holder, and a Hall of Famer. To that list, I now add "published author."

You may or may not be impressed by my accolades, but the work ethic, consistency, and discipline it took to achieve them are worthy of respect. At any rate, please do not allow my success to intimidate you or lead you to assume that I will not be relatable. I was once afraid of failure, success, and criticism. At first, I was oblivious to my true potential, and I allowed doubt, the opinions of others, and personal insecurities to limit me. Throughout this book, I will explain how I overcame these obstacles. No matter what, in my heart, I will always be that young, skinny, tall kid who loves learning, spending time with family, playing games, listening to music, and enjoying sporting events. But above all, I find joy in making people smile and helping them see the power within themselves.

In this social media age, too many people only show their highlight reel, but that is understandable. Throughout time, people have admired, idolized, and gravitated towards individuals or groups who have attained certain accolades and recognition in the realms of finance (material wealth), athletics (physical and mental wealth), and lifestyle (wealth of self-sufficiency and freedom). I listed my achievements earlier, but now I will list the failures and obstacles that came before them:

1. My high school basketball coaches cut me from the team TWICE!
2. When I finally made my high school basketball team, I embarrassingly missed my first in-game dunk attempt in front of a packed crowd on my father's birthday.
3. I failed my first two college exams, and I wanted to quit after my first semester!
4. After one month in college, I decided to change the major that I had planned for since the seventh grade.
5. During my sophomore year in college, I fractured my ankle and could not run for 13 weeks. This placed my athletic career and scholarships in jeopardy.
6. A dream internship in San Diego, California that I had assumed would be a guaranteed acceptance rejected my application.

7. To earn my master's degree, I narrowly passed my required courses. I did not find out that I had officially graduated until an entire week after the graduation ceremonies.
8. As a salesperson, people have told me "No" or utterly lied to me hundreds of times.
9. I lost by 300 votes in my political campaign to become a school board member.
10. Although I had a legitimate opportunity, I failed to qualify for the 2020 Olympic Games.

I will elaborate on these situations with detailed stories throughout the book.

Question Everything?

As a human being, it is your duty and your right to ask questions. When you do not question the ideas, things, patterns, or people around you, you become an ignorant follower. According to Merriam-Webster.com, the word "ignorance" means "lack of knowledge, education, or awareness." I will use sheep as an example here. No matter what is going on in the world around them, sheep blindly follow the crowd, even if they are being led to their demise. However, history has shown us that those who ask questions and do not blindly follow the crowd are the ones who will be remembered and revered by generations to come. Which option will you choose?

"Curiosity killed the cat" is a popular saying. I would like to add the comical myth that the cat had nine lives. The cat learned from its previous lives, and it eventually was resurrected to become an unstoppable and ferocious lion! The moral of the story here is that you live and learn. Please contemplate the point I am making here. You do not have to stop living to learn your lessons. Be courageous, try new experiences, know that you can bounce back from just about anything, and accept that there are lessons to be learned from everything you do and go through.

To further explain the importance of questioning, let's analyze the "Mom and the Ham" parable. My mother originally told me this story as we were discussing statistics and the things that most people surprisingly do because of unconscious habits. Later, I saw the same story in Dr. J.C. Baker's first book, *Common Cents: How Much Does It Cost?*

There was a mother that cut off the ends of her ham before she cooked for holidays. Her daughter asked, "Mom why do you cut the ends of your ham off?"

The mother answers, "Well my mom always did it and I learned from her."

The child says, "Can we ask grandmother why she did?"

The mother says, "Of course!"

The mother goes to ask the grandmother, "Mother why do you cut the ends off of the holiday ham?"

The Grandmother replied, "I watched my mom cut the ends off for years and that is how I learned."

The daughter with a greater curiosity asks, "Can we speak to my great grandmother?"

The mother agrees they should. Once they arrive at the great-grandmother's house, they ask, "Great Grandma why do you cut the ends off of the holiday ham?"

Great Grandma replies, "It was the only way the ham would fit into my pan."

Think about all the ham they had wasted for decades after getting larger pans! All because it took generations for a child to finally ask "Why?" Please do not take this lesson lightly. Question Everything!

In this same story, other scenarios could have occurred. The child could have never asked her mom "Why?" and just continued the same tradition of wasting food, or the child could have received a completely different answer to her question. The mother could have gotten defensive and triggered when her child asked "Why?" and then angrily replied, "Because that's how our family does it, and you should do the same!"

I will elaborate on this crucial point further, as culturally in America and other parts of the world, many can relate to this.

A parent, who is generally a student's first teacher, gives their child an instruction to follow. An instruction could be: "Every Tuesday at 7:00 PM I need you to take the trash out." Out of genuine curiosity, the child then asks "Why?" The parent's typical response is "Because I said so" or "Don't get smart with me" in an authoritative tone. It is my belief that these types of responses are used too often as an evasion tactics or flexes of power that eventually hurts everyone involved. The parent's inability or un-willingness to explain the reasoning now limits the child's ability and opportunity to learn.

The child now develops a mindset to not question authority and just do what authoritative figures tell them. If children view their peers as authorities due to factors such as admiration or intimidation, they will blindly follow instructions that could be misleading or malicious. Authoritative figures also include those projecting opinions on mainstream and social media, the government, and law enforcement. Just like all institutions throughout the history of time, these systems contain certain levels of corruption and biased information that is eventually manipulated to control the minds of the masses. Notice how this relates to the traditional school system, where many students' curiosity is suppressed, as they are programmed to only follow directions given by authoritative figures.

It would be unwise to give unquestionable power to any person, group, or system. Having and using the ability to ask questions gives a sense of power. Be sure to maintain this power in all areas of life.

Change the Way You Ask Questions

Yes, it makes sense to question everything, but there are more effective ways to ask questions than just saying "Why?" Chris Voss, a former FBI negotiator who now coaches sales and negotiation on a global stage, teaches how the question "Why?" brings about an emotional response that stems from childhood. When you were barely old enough to tie your own shoes and you did something wrong or that your parents did not like, they would angrily ask "Why would you do that!?" This now triggers you and most people in America to become defensive, regardless of age.

With this information, I will now teach you how to ask better questions to gain better responses. Since the other person's response is likely to reflect your tone, be sure to maintain a calm demeanor. Then, change your typical "Whys" to "Whats." Here are some examples:

"Why did you do that?" translates to **"What caused you to take that action?"**

"Why are you...?" translates to **"What is the reason for...?"**

"Why can't you just...?" translates to **"What is stopping you from...?"**

Pay close attention to the different conversations and interactions you have throughout your days. Notice when you would usually ask someone "Why?" and be creative to rephrase your question by starting with the word "What."

Four Levels of Competence

Understand that in life, you are embarking on a journey full of learning. In this book, you will learn from my perspectives, based on my life's trials and tribulations. The advice I give is intended to help you think, plan, and avoid careless or costly mistakes. When learning and implementing something new, you must understand that it is not an overnight process. Rather, it will require different levels of patience. When we first encounter new information, whether it's through reading, watching, listening, or experiencing something, what we are meant to learn or understand may not click at that exact moment. It could take years before what you learned truly makes sense to you.

Below is the psychological process broken down into four phases which I learned from one of my professional track coaches, Dwight Phillips:

1. First, you are **unconsciously incompetent**. This is simply because nobody has ever taught you the best way of thinking or accomplishing a task.
2. The second level of learning is becoming **consciously incompetent**. This means that now you know when you are doing a task the wrong way, but you have not fully corrected your mistakes.
3. The third level is becoming **consciously competent**. You are aware of all your actions, but you have not had enough repetitions to execute them properly and consistently without having to think about them carefully.
4. Finally, we all strive to become **unconsciously competent**. You no longer think too hard about your actions because they have become automatic.

Self-Reflection Questions

The following questions aid us in our self-development:

- Who am I?
- Who do I want to become?
- What do I want to be remembered for?
- What do I truly desire?
- Who is in control of my life and my thoughts?
- What am I consuming (through my ears, eyes, & mouth)?
- Where am I spending my time, money, and energy?
- What must I do to achieve my goals?
- What does success look like to me?
- Who are my mentors? *Are they leading me to where I want to go?*
- What am I passionate about?
- What are my addictions and habits? *Are they positive or negative? Are they healthy or unhealthy?*
- Who am I following and listening to, including social media, music, and real life? *Is it productive?*
- When I have conversations, what are the topics? *Am I gossiping or growing?*
- What advice would I give my younger self? *In two words? In one sentence? In one paragraph?*

CHAPTER 2

Adolescence

Influences

What influences a child? Their parents, family, friends, school, neighborhood, and media (television, music, social platforms) are their chief influencers. Ask yourself, "What qualities, habits, and phrases do my parents, family, and friends possess? Which ones are good and which ones are bad?" Once you are aware of these things and you have labeled them, which ones will you choose to emulate? Which ones will you avoid?

Childhood

Everyone, no matter how grown up they are now, was once a child. Even on your 100th birthday, you will still be your parents' child, whether they are still on Earth or not. In this chapter, I will expound on my upbringing and the lessons I learned during and after. This will not be a boring biography, as you will only read about the experiences that have meaningful lessons attached to them.

When I was four years old, my parents enrolled me in pre-K at a local private school; this is the origin of how I was so young compared to my classmates in future years. After only two weeks, my teachers realized I was smart enough to immediately jump to kindergarten and my parents agreed. Academically, socially, and physically, this was an easy transition as my above-average grades and height helped me to fit in with my older classmates.

While living in Hampton, Virginia, I played soccer as my first sport. With no exaggeration, I was one of the best in my age group at every position except goalie. Sadly, this was during a time when I cared too much about what my older cousins thought. They labeled soccer as non-masculine, which then led me to quit so I could gain their approval. After quitting soccer, I increased my focus on only playing organized football and basketball. Eventually, basketball became my primary sport and passion.

Let us pause here for some crucial advice in the form of a letter to my younger self:

Dear Kenny,

STOP LIMITING YOURSELF BASED ON WHAT PEOPLE THINK ABOUT YOU! Love yourself and embrace who you were created to be. If you love to do something, do it. If you love someone, express it. Be courageous and unworried about the belittling opinions of others. When people talk about you in a negative way, it is because they have a problem within themselves. Understand that we all have flaws and internal battles to overcome, but do not let that stop you from becoming the best version of yourself. Even if others do not see your vision, go for it anyway.

I understand the basic human need and desire to fit in for external validation. There was a time in my life when I sought it from the wrong people and places. But it is imperative that you reach a point where you no longer seek it from those who do not truly support you. I am referring to the people who do not know or love the real you and your many layers. However, there may be moments when the people who love you will even try to limit your growth because they are afraid of change. I am here to tell you that change is uncomfortable but necessary and inevitable. Continue to always change for the better.

Now, there will be people who try to "help" you along your life journey. But you must have the discernment to determine if this help is good or bad.

Typically, it depends on the specific advice, action, or thing that is being offered. One of my mentors, Derek Williams (aka MR1NF1N1TY), has stated: "Never take advice from anyone in any field that has not accomplished the results you are seeking to produce." This means that if they have not been in your shoes before or helped others who are like you, do not follow their advice. However, people who have not achieved the results you want are still a benefit. Why? Because you can listen to them and learn what NOT to do!

Sincerely,

Kenny Glenn, Success Coach and Entrepreneur

Positive Role Models

What benefits (physical, mental, and spiritual) have your parents or guardians provided you? If you grew up without your father, or if he was not a positive role model, which man or men in your life can teach you important life skills, lessons, and words of wisdom? If you grew up without your mother or if she was not a positive role model, which woman or women in your life can teach you important life skills, lessons, and words of wisdom?

This is the part of the book where I elaborate on how beneficial my parents were in molding me. As a man, I will specifically focus more on my father, as he was my first and closest male role model. I understand the importance of any child growing up with their father, and thankfully, I had mine in my household to show me how to become a man. Plus, having both parents in the house allowed for a healthy balance of masculine and feminine energy. I have friends and family who grew up without their fathers or mothers, and I now see how it affected and still affects them. However, they still looked to someone to teach them and help them become who they are today.

Even outside of my father, I had men who looked like me and exemplified what I wanted to become. This included teachers, administrators, and older men I met on the basketball court or in my neighborhood. Every day while in middle and high school I heard my assistant principal on the building-wide intercom as he gave important announcements. Each time, he would finish with a powerful saying: "Everybody wants to change the world, but nobody wants to change themselves. BE THE CHANGE YOU WANT TO SEE IN THE WORLD." When a student lacks these types of positive influences, it creates an easier path towards being weighed down by harmful temptations and adopting negative stereotypes.

My father was my first soccer, football, and basketball coach. He taught me the importance of waking up early and providing for myself and my family, which meant much more than just finances. He taught me how to love and protect women, how to finesse and be smooth, how to dress with style, how to walk like a boss, how to cook, how to believe in myself, how to drive, and many more valuable lessons! He also took me to church and instilled the fact that God has a plan for my life. He ensured that I stayed out of serious trouble by instilling no-nonsense consequences. He also introduced my sister and me to the value of credit and the greatest movie of all time, *The Matrix*.

Due to my father's active military status, there were times during my early years when he was away from home for extended periods of time. I vividly remember my father being overseas on a naval ship for six months when I was in the fifth grade. This meant he would miss the holidays of Christmas and New Year's Day. It was the first and only time I could remember that being the case. I missed my father while he was gone, and this is when I got in the most trouble at school. I stole money, acted out in class, and got suspended. But even as a nine-year-old kid, I somehow knew that my mother would be more lenient with the punishments she gave; this seems common in mother-son relationships.

14

For example, if she said I was grounded for three months without certain privileges, I often returned to my normal activities after only a couple of weeks.

Eventually, my father returned home and retired from the military after 20 years of service. At his retirement ceremony, someone asked me if I was next. Since I was only nine years old, I did not know how to respond. My father jumped in and replied, "Nope. My son is going to college." That statement put the expectation in my mind to continuously achieve high academic goals so I could get to college and succeed.

My father was always supportive. Whether he would physically come to my sporting events or not, he would always call me to give words of encouragement, even if he needed to leave a voicemail. "Smoke deez cats" is a phrase he would frequently say. Then after my competitions, he would congratulate me and give advice on how I could improve. To grow my confidence, he would repeatedly say to me: "Go out there and be fearless. No matter what happens, nobody can take anything away from you. Your loved ones will still love you, and your birthday will still be celebrated." This applies to all situations where courage and confidence are necessary, including athletics, job interviews, and public speaking. On my first day of college, he assured me via text that there was nothing my professors could throw my way that I did not have the tools to handle.

My mother also strongly believed in me, and she was satisfied whenever I gave my best effort. However, academically and behaviorally, she refused to let me be average in the classroom. She and my teachers knew I was special because if all my other classmates were doing something wrong, and then I decided to join in, I would be the one to get in trouble. The famous line from Black mothers that I heard her say many times was: "I don't care what the other kids were doing. Those other kids are not mine. I raised you better, and I expect you to show it."

Often, if I really wanted a new pair of shoes or a new video game, my mother would agree to help me get it by paying for half of the expense. I could write another book full of examples of the love and support that she gave which was instrumental in shaping who I am today. However, I will keep it short, as I know mothers tend to overly coddle their sons, similar to the way fathers tend to treat their daughters.

My advice to boys and girls, men and women, fathers and mothers, is to recognize the importance of each other and show respect. It takes a village to properly raise a child, but it all starts at home. We need the best version of each other to build a brighter future filled with highly educated families and individuals. Find and follow positive examples of who you want to become, not who society will try to create you to be.

The Benefits of Teacher Relationships

The teacher I must mention and expound upon is my middle school science teacher, Ms. Veronica Dean! In my opinion, she is the greatest science and robotics teacher that the world has ever seen! She gifted me and many other students with academic opportunities to grow, learn, and create lifelong friendships outside of the classroom. Although she is a bit quirky and some students may dislike her strict rules, I am beyond thankful for her. She cultivated after-school programs to introduce students to the fun and tangible uses of STEM (science, technology, engineering, and math). In those programs, we built Lego robots, toothpick bridges, and mousetrap racecars. She also led a group of us to compete on an academic team against other local schools. This was quite similar to physical sports, but we were showcasing our brainpower instead of our athletic abilities.

Ms. Dean also recommended to my parents the option to participate in summer programs at the University of Cincinnati that were offered to middle and high school students. These programs were designed to give marginalized students the opportunity to take classes on a college campus, meet faculty, prepare for college entrance exams, and enhance their skills in the subjects of math, science, and writing.

I absolutely did not want to attend these programs for multiple obvious reasons as a kid in the seventh and eighth grades. The summer program always started on the exact date or week of my birthday. I also did not want to spend eight weeks of my summer sitting in classes learning about subjects that came easy to me. I much preferred playing basketball at any time, on any day, or staying up all night playing video games! However, since my parents were future-oriented and wanted the best for me, they demanded that I participate.

I did not agree with my parents back then, but now I see that they were only providing me with more options to succeed while ensuring my academic skills were always on point. I vividly remember my mother telling me that we could not afford college. This program would be the path towards scholarships before I even knew what those were. Thanks to these programs I made lifelong friends with future engineers from different high schools around the state of Ohio, such as Christopher Steward. I was also able to create some hilarious and unforgettable memories! For example, my neighbor Joe Abrams and I would walk around campus to ask professors and students for spare change so we could buy ice cream.

Dear Kenny,

Connect with your teachers and administrators on a personal level and ask them questions about their life journeys. Find out the people they know who can help you reach your goals. I still talk to some of my teachers from middle school, high school, and college. My past teachers have written letters of recommendation for me, helped with my political campaign, given me access to workout facilities, and more! They have helped me in so many ways that I do not know where I would be without them.

Even teachers with whom I had no classes have also helped me based on my positive reputation! Huge shoutout to all those who continue to support me along my post-graduation journey.

Also, do not waste your summers! I know this is your time to relax and have fun in the sun, but this is also your opportunity to stay sharp in the classroom and in athletics. Strike a healthy balance. Use your time and resources wisely.

Sincerely,

Kenny Glenn, Success Coach and Entrepreneur

Eighth Grade

During my eighth-grade year, I tried out for my middle school basketball team and made it! However, I only scored three points the whole season due to my lack of courage and my fear of criticism. I eventually had to break these shackles, and throughout this book, I will elaborate on how I did it.

I always had the hustle and spirit of an entrepreneur, and I proved this in the eighth grade. It was sparked by my father when he said, "I will never buy my kids a game system." I was hurt by this statement because of how badly I wanted an Xbox 360! This caused me to learn how to save all the money I received from holidays plus what I earned from cutting grass and shoveling snow for our elderly neighbors. His statement also sparked me to create another business venture as I began selling candy at school to earn enough money to purchase my own gaming system.

Dear Kenny,

Please never see yourself as dumb or unable to understand business and numbers. In the eighth grade, I knew more about business than some college graduates. Learn the basics of business so you can think like a business owner and know how capitalism works. Learning and understanding the Six Secrets of Persuasion will be a major help; so much so that it will feel like a cheat code!

Sincerely,

Kenny Glenn, Success Coach and Entrepreneur

The Six Secrets of Persuasion

Dr. J.C. Baker has taught me and business owners all over the world about these persuasive techniques. They were originally theorized by Dr. Robert Cialdini. These concepts are quite simple when you break them down. They can be applied in your personal and professional interactions. The best way to remember them is with the acronym, C. CARLS. After explaining the Six Secrets of Persuasion, I will explain how I used them in the eighth grade.

1. **Consensus** is a general agreement, including customer reviews of people, products, and services.
2. **Consistency** involves repeated or normalized behavior or qualities. For example, McDonald's food tastes the same at every location in the chain. Another example is if you always do, say, or wear the same things, people will come to expect it.
3. **Authorities** are people or organizations having power or control in a particular area. For example, people are more

19

    likely to listen to experienced professionals before listen-
    ing to amateurs because of authority and experience.

4. **Reciprocity** is the practice of exchanging things with others for mutual benefit. Give people respect without being
   asked, and they are more likely to respect you in return.

5. **Liking** is arguably the strongest of the six. People listen to
   and buy from people or companies that they like for
   various reasons.

6. **Scarcity** refers to the low availability or quantity of
   options. Having limited choices or seeing/hearing
   phrases like "While supplies last" makes people buy
   sooner than later.

First, I noticed that Meijer sold large bags of regular and sour
Starburst for $2 each. I purchased a bag and opened it to count
how many pieces of candy were inside. To my surprise, the total
number was 80! This surprised me because if you purchased the
$1 pack at the register, they only gave you 12 pieces. This sparked
the idea of pricing each piece for ten cents or selling a bundle of
ten pieces for $1. By selling each bag in full I would earn $8. Then,
by subtracting the $2 it cost me to buy the candy, I would profit
$6 per bag. I knew my audience of eighth-grade students in school
for seven hours a day would purchase what I had. I was well-liked,
and I did not hate on anybody else's hustle or way of thinking
(LIKING and RECIPROCITY). I also knew there were no other
sources for students to get my product while we were in school
(SCARCITY and AUTHORITY). I must also write that I was
certainly not given permission or allowed to sell anything on
school property. However, I am a finesser with morals. I can earn
or save money in ways that do not harm others. As an honors
student who did not get into any serious trouble, teachers did not
have me on their "suspect" radar. They were not keeping a close

eye on me as I sold candy. I had a top customer every day who rode the same bus to school with me. He purchased $2 worth of candy every single morning and he knew I would have them (CONSISTENCY). I also began to sell gum for 25 cents apiece. We all know that once you open a pack of gum publicly, every single person wants a piece (CONSENSUS)! I discovered that only 15 pieces of gum were inside the typical packs sold at gas stations and grocery store registers. However, I knew there had to be a way to get more pieces for the same $1 price tag. This is when I discovered that Dollar Tree sold four-packs with five pieces of gum per pack in a plastic bundle for $1. This meant that for the same price, I could get 20 pieces instead of only 15.

Now in this same eighth grade school year, I was eventually labeled as a disruptive class clown. I did this to fit in socially, and my grades began to slip because of it. Yes, I was smart and in honors classes, but those labels were not seen as cool among my social group. Although I was on the basketball team, I barely got in the game. I was also two years younger than my peers, and they made constant jokes about my age. Dr. Jawanza Kunjufu explains this reality within young students as this is a societal problem of valuing popularity over intelligence. I do not remember my teachers directly attempting to correct my behavior by having private conversations with me. I thought I was getting away with my antics until my teachers told my parents about my behavior at Parent-Teacher Conference Night.

That night, my father had an intense talk with me and said I needed to get my act together. He explained that I was too smart to be fooling around and that I was embarrassing him by doing so. We looked just alike and had the same first and last name. Anything I did would affect his reputation and how people viewed him as a father. Until that moment, I had never thought about how I was carrying his and our family's legacy. Next, my mother came to me and used her feminine energy to cheer me up. She said that if I stayed out of trouble and got the grades that she knew I could achieve, she would reward me. The reward was $50 per A, but only $5 per B.

Dear Kenny,

I know that not every student has someone who financially rewards them for their good grades in the short term. But I am here to let you know that good grades will get you paid in the long run. Teachers will treat you better (social capital), and organizations will give you scholarships to make college less expensive (financial capital).

Sincerely,

Kenny Glenn, Success Coach and Entrepreneur

The Power of Sound

My father got me hip to the jams and broke down the deeper meaning of certain lyrics! When I say jams, I am referring to the hip-hop and R&B music that was released in the 1980s, 1990s, and early 2000s, as well as the soul music from the 1970s. He made sure the music he played was the clean version so I would not become comfortable with using foul language. My mother got me hip to artists like Luther Vandross, Stevie Wonder, Michael Jackson, and Lionel Richie. In the eighth grade, I took a music class and learned about some of the very first rap songs by artists like Grandmaster Flash and the Sugarhill Gang. Combined, these are the reasons why I still intently listen to the lyrics when it comes to music. Fast forward to today, if a musical artist is singing or rapping about stupidity, I AM NOT LISTENING! In the words of Common in the song "The 6th Sense," "If I don't like it, I don't like it. That don't mean that I'm hating." I do not care how popular a song might be because I know the music industry tries to program us to listen to and buy hot garbage.

IT IS COOL TO MARCH TO YOUR OWN BEAT! Literally and figuratively. I remember trying to force myself to like the music they play in clubs or that some of my teammates would listen to. But the truth was that I loved "real" music! Music that expressed love and vulnerability. Music that had wordplay and master lyricism. Not mumble rap or music that talked about disrespecting women or causing harm to anyone.

The power of sound dictates how we receive information and how we feel. Music and words have vibrations and frequencies attached to them that shift our energy. You can change a person's mood and thoughts by playing certain songs or types of music. You could also create this change by the words you speak to them and how you say those words. Songs, videos, movies, podcasts, and audiobooks are filled with information and opportunities to learn by listening and watching. Will you listen to the negative or the positive vibrations?

Dear Kenny,

Feed your soul and your mind with positive sounds. Be conscious of what you allow to enter your ears. It is okay and beneficial to listen to some jazz, piano, or baroque music to calm you down and joyfully lift your spirit. Most young listeners look at musicians as role models. There are some musicians we should just listen to and respect their craft while leaving their personal lives out of it. If you choose to dive deeper into the personal lives of musicians, be conscious of what you choose to adopt from how they carry themselves.

The music that is predominantly marketed towards you is filled with the promotion of sex, drugs, and death. Too often, the musical artist is just a middleman salesperson with a good beat and a catchy saying. But if you dissect the lyrics, many of them are leading you in the wrong direction. Some musicians will tell you to spend all your money, trust no one, promote violence against your own people as a viable solution, sell or do harmful drugs, and to only think about sex. That way of living is too risky an unsustainable. But meanwhile, those same musicians are peacefully at home saving their money while also being happily married and raising their children. They are not even living the life they are rapping about or posting on social media! But as listeners, we are constantly being programmed by repetition: the number of times we watch, listen, and ingest their music, as well as the fast and flashy lifestyles they portray. We give these entertainers millions of dollars while we as listeners stay in the rat race of living paycheck to paycheck, and always spending our money on escapism. We know every single word to their songs but soon as someone attempts to educate us on the things that matter, we suddenly cannot hear.

Imagine me screaming these next two sentences: WHO CARES IF YOU KNOW ALL THE WORDS TO THE NEWEST TRAP SONG? DOES IT EVEN MATTER?

Most of us listen to music when we are in the car or whenever we wear headphones. But have you ever attempted to listen to something else? You can listen to old and new songs on repeat, and nothing will change. You might be wondering, "Well if I do not listen to music, then what will I listen to?" You can listen to audiobooks, podcasts, and interviews with people you would label as successful or knowledgeable. The information they give can improve how you think and conduct yourself. Since everything starts with a thought, these different choices can change your life for the better! I am not saying that you must completely give up listening to music in the car or at any other point of your day, but sometimes switch it up. Listening to podcasts has improved my life with the information I have learned and the people I have connected with.

Sincerely,

Kenny Glenn, Success Coach and Entrepreneur

SECTION 2:
HIGH SCHOOL

Everybody has a different puzzle, man.
You just got to figure out your own puzzle.

— Kobe Bryant

CHAPTER 3

Postsecondary Preparation

High school is a microcosm of life. Use your time wisely before graduating to the next level.

— Kenny Glenn

Life is a game, and in America, high school is another level for students to complete before being taken seriously. Like the board game *Monopoly*, there are prices you must pay to get where you want to go, even the prices you do not want to pay. You will read about my personal experience in Chapter 4. This chapter is composed of the advice I give to most high school students.

Before I dive into the specific points of preparation, I urge each high school student to ask themselves and answer the self-assessment questions listed on the next couple of pages. If you are reading this as a high school graduate, use these same questions for high school students that you mentor or encounter.

1. What do I genuinely want to do after high school?

- Do not give the generic answer that you think your peers, parents, or teachers will accept as "good." Be honest and carve your own path.
- What are the people I want to be like doing on a day-to-day basis? What are they wearing? What are they reading? What information are they constantly consuming and from what sources? What did they do to get to where they are?

2. What is currently available to help make sure that what I want to do after high school becomes a reality?

- Examples include mentors, counselors, teachers, and alumni who have done it already.
- Books and videos also explain certain processes.

3. What are my academic goals?

- Which classes are my favorite and least favorite?
- Which classes am I best at and worst at?
    - Is this because of my teachers, my natural ability, or my level of effort?
    - What actions have I taken to get the help I need?
    - Do I have access to a tutor?
- Do I plan to go to college? If so, where?
    - Public or private?
    - In-state or out-of-state?
    - How much will it cost?
    - How will I pay for it (FAFSA, scholarships, loans, etc.)?
    - What GPA and test scores do I need?

4. What are my extracurricular goals?

- Improvement in the arts (music, cooking, photography, etc.)?
- Athletics (specific statistics and college offers)?
- Increase network and social interaction (organizations, community service, etc.)?
- Employment (future career advancement or short-term financial necessity)

5. What are the top three distractions that take time and energy away from achieving my goals?

- Activities include flirting, social media, and too much unnecessary time on the phone.
- Emotional concerns might include trouble in the home or trouble in the neighborhood.
- Personal responsibilities might include taking care of my family and working a job because I need the money.

6. Do my family and friends support and respect my dreams and the sacrifices I must make to achieve them?

Paying Attention to Your Environment

Our environment is stronger than nature, and we unconsciously follow and think like those we interact with most. Although you may have a large network of people you associate with, we become the average of the five people we spend most of our time with. When you are a student, this includes parents, siblings, friends, classmates, teammates, teachers, community members, and even yourself. This also includes people we have not met in real life, like celebrities we admire from music, movies, and social

29

media. Notice that wealthy people hang out with wealthy people. Engineers hang out with engineers. Crackheads hang with crackheads! What does who you spend the most time with say about you?

Even with these generic labels, you do not have to do everything with the same person or group of people, as we are multifaceted beings with different interests and hobbies. If you do everything with the same people, you are limiting yourself and the benefits of having an expansive network. No matter how much you and someone else have in common, no two people are exactly alike, not even identical twins. To serve as an example, in high school, I was an honor roll student on the academic team and the basketball team. I was well above average height, but during ninth and tenth grade, my closest friends were shorter than average. In college, I was on the track team, but I hung out with athletes from other sports and even students who were not college athletes. Today, I am a Black man, but I spend time with friends from all different backgrounds and nationalities, regardless of their religious or political affiliations.

With this awareness, you now can design your own path. I have family members who have been shot or have thrown away their futures because of drugs and incarceration. On the flip side, I also have cousins who have great jobs or profitable businesses, travel all around the world, and live peacefully. Regardless of who your parents are or who you are related to, as said by Jeremy Anderson, "Your DNA does not determine your destiny; your decisions do." Who will you choose to follow and interact with?

Leveraging School and Defining Success

High school simply provides the foundational knowledge that our current society tells us we need. However, if students do not leverage school correctly, they will view it as a waste of time. It is wise for you to figure out who lives the life you want and then learn from those people with intention. Teachers may not teach this within their curriculum, but teachers might have the perfect network of resources to still help you reach your goals. Use school and the opportunities it presents to develop skills that will help you reach your definition of success—skills like public speaking, critical thinking, fostering meaningful relationships, and working with teams. Allow me to delve into defining success for yourself.

People may try to tell you what success is, but success is a word you must define for yourself. It takes time and patience to achieve your definition of success, as nothing happens overnight. A woman is pregnant nine months before she pushes her baby out into the world. Not nine days or nine weeks, but nine months! This is an example to show that it takes time to grow and bring your ideas into reality. We live in an impatient society that wants things to be seedless, microwaved, and shipped to us ASAP. But the best and healthiest food had to be planted by seeds. Then, it took time, patience, and cultivation for those seeds to grow into what we can use for food. During the growth phase, the seeds had to burst and go through the pain of being uncomfortable so they could become what they were destined to be. Then, we all know that food is best when cooked in the oven or on the stove. This takes longer than the microwave, but it is worth the wait for many reasons. Use this seed analogy for your journey towards success.

We must also realize that success is not an accident. In the book *Outliers*, the author Malcolm Gladwell dissects the many factors that attribute to someone being successful. Decisions that your ancestors made, the city you live in, or someone that you randomly met, all come together to attribute to your success. But no matter what, it comes down to the choices you make with your available options. What I want you to focus on is being grateful for everything you have and everything that has ever happened to you. Even if that thing is typically labeled as bad, find a way to see the good and use it for your benefit.

Did you grow up in a bad neighborhood? GOOD! You were able to learn from your environment and translate those lessons into bettering your future. Did someone break your heart? GOOD! Now, you can learn how to better love yourself. Your parents did not go to college? GOOD! You can be the first in your family to attend, graduate, and leave an impactful legacy. I can give more examples, but hopefully, you get the point.

The Illusion of Time

Two critical preparation points are the Illusion of Time and the 4 Es of Postgrad Options. I created this phrase during a school board meeting when I noticed how quickly four years of school can fly by! When students enter their first year, they think and feel like they have all the time in the world to figure out what they are going to do. But then, all too often, they arrive at senior year more quickly than they realized, still without any concrete plans. Here is a simple grade-by-grade breakdown to help students capitalize on their time.

Ninth Grade

This is the year students set their foundations. Your GPA and the type of classes you will take for the rest of your high school career are dependent on this year. Do your absolute best to avoid low grades or failed classes. You do not want to put yourself in a hole and then play catch up while your classes become more difficult.

Build a positive reputation for yourself in terms of academics and character, and let it follow you throughout your remaining school years. Build positive relationships with the faculty and staff, including teachers, administrators, coaches, and guidance counselors. Not everyone will be helpful, but you will find people who recognize your potential and look out for you. They will be the ones who will write strong recommendations for you later.

Tenth Grade

Depending on the city and state you live in, this is the year you can make a life-changing decision! In my hometown of Cincinnati, and other cities in Ohio, students can choose to attend a vocational school that their high school will pay for. For two years, you could go learn a trade like HVAC, plumbing, or welding. Think about what your interests are and the problems you can help solve.

Let me be the one to break the stigma. Contrary to the common assumption, a student who chooses to attend a vocational school while they are in high school can still go to college afterward! Here is a story about how important this decision really is.

My friend and high school teammate, Andrew Wilfong, chose to follow his dreams of becoming a Registered Nurse and playing college basketball. He was also a class clown who made the jump from special education classes to honors courses, which meant that he had the option of going either route. He chose to not attend Great Oaks, which was the trade school option for juniors and seniors at our high school. Three years after graduating from high school, he had accumulated over $40,000 in student loan debt after switching colleges multiple times while chasing a career he did not truly love. The only reason he gravitated towards nursing is because his mother chose that career path. He eventually found his passion in HVAC and had to pay another institution so he could master it and become certified. My friend's story also illustrates that the final decision is always yours and that you should never be afraid to redirect yourself if you think it would be in your best interest long-term. The change was better late than never. Today, he earns an above-average salary as one of the top HVAC specialists in Cincinnati.

Now, what if he had chosen to attend a vocational school in high school? Since he wanted to be a nurse, it would have been wise to attend Great Oaks for that specialty. While at Great Oaks, he could have realized how much he disliked nursing and switched his focus to learning about HVAC. Then, he could have become certified and received multiple job opportunities right after high school! On top of that, he still could have gone to college to play basketball while having the opportunity to get paid for his HVAC skills.

Eleventh Grade

This is the last year that colleges truly pay attention to on your transcript for admission to their institution. They will look at your GPA from this year and previous years, as well as the types of classes you plan to take during your senior year. For athletes seeking to play at the college level, this is an especially important season. By doing your absolute best as a junior, you place yourself under less pressure as a senior.

Twelfth Grade

THIS IS IT! After this, you will no longer be treated the same. As a graduate and an adult, you will be swimming in "the real world." Enjoy this last year with your classmates and teachers because once you graduate, it may be decades before you see most of them again. Some relationships will last a lifetime. Others will not. You will realize that some of your "friends" were only friends because you saw them every day. Just remember that it is perfectly normal to grow apart. Cherish the memories but do not lose sight of what is best for your future.

After you graduate, it is important to know that there will be many instances where you will wonder "How come no one told me this while I was in school!?" Regardless of what you were or were not taught, it is your responsibility to never stop learning.

If you are going to college, think about financial aid. Complete the FAFSA as early as possible. You should be applying for scholarships every week. It is also a great idea to check in with the guidance office regularly to see if they have useful ideas.

If you are not going to college, start planning out your financial situation. Here are some sample questions to answer:

- Where will I live after graduation?
- Where will I work?
- How much longer can my parent(s) cover me on their health, dental, and vision insurance?
- Out of all my classmates, who are my closest friends?

The 4 Es of Postgrad Options

Students must plan for what they will do with their lives after high school graduation. They have four basic options:

1. **Enrollment**
2. **Employment**
3. **Entrepreneurship**
4. **Enlistment**

E1: Enrollment

Students have the option to enroll in college or trade school after graduating from high school. I advise all students to take considerable time to think about why they want to attend college or trade school. Trade school is a more direct path because the student must focus on a specialty, such as nursing, electrical work, or construction. College can be a vague choice if you choose a major outside of engineering, law, medicine, or business. Some people may blindly tell you to "go to college," but I am not one of those people. This is a thought that goes through the minds of some students: "Why go to college? I see so many graduates complain about and get stressed out over student loan debt, or some say they could have obtained their jobs without college." But beware. The opposite is also true, as many people wish they would have gone to college for the experience and vast network. We all know college can be expensive without scholarships and grants, but it is worth it if you leverage it correctly.

My advice here is to find current college students and college graduates and ask them questions that will expose the truth about their personal experiences. Do not just ask them about the fun stuff. Ask about the finances (scholarships, loans, and current debt), their application processes, the required ACT or SAT scores, their majors, their course loads, the greatest lessons they have learned, and if they have any regrets. **If you choose to go to college, be sure you are going for the right reasons and with the mission to receive a positive return on your investment (money, time, and energy).**

Here are the main reasons that students attend college:

- Students want more time to mature while removing uncertainty. Even with a plan, many high school graduates are not sure what they truly want to do with their lives.
- Societal pressure says you will be a failure if you do not attend college.
- Students want to meet and network with past, present, and future students and staff. Students are surrounded by people who are on the same quest, as well as university faculty and staff who have already gone through the college process and want to help current students.
- They want the dream and the experience. Living on a college campus is a student's opportunity to experience freedom by living in a new environment and being less restricted by the rules of their parents. Students also want to go through the "struggle of a poor college student," attend parties, live in dorm rooms, eat in buffet-style dining halls, eat Ramen noodles, pull all-nighters for papers and exams, and join organizations.
- They want to specialize in a field of study and expand their career options. Ultimately, students are rewarded with degrees and employment.
- Athletes want to continue with their sports.

E2: Employment

Becoming an employee is what school was created for. The current school system is still modeled in this way, and the curriculum supports that. I am not bashing anyone who chooses the employee route. Businesses need employees, and employees need what businesses offer them, which includes experience, guaranteed income, paid vacations, healthcare insurance, retirement benefits, networking, and a sense of belonging.

Look at being an employee as an opportunity for being paid to learn. With anything you do at your job, you are acquiring skills and learning a certain way of accomplishing tasks. For many entrepreneurs, being an employee was their first "investor." They used the dollars they earned from their job to pay for what they needed to become an entrepreneur.

E3: Entrepreneurship

According to Oxford Languages (The Oxford English Dictionary), an entrepreneur is "a person who organizes and operates a business or businesses, taking on greater than normal financial risks in order to do so." If you choose this route, be sure to have a plan, analyze your risks, and know you are getting on the wildest emotional roller coaster of your life: the field of sales. A business owner either sells products, services, or both. Sales run the world because everything we consume is sold to us by someone or some entity. It is also important to know the hilarious fact that ANYTHING can be sold. Companies have earned millions of dollars from selling pet rocks. As an entrepreneur, you have tons of options to choose from! Every year, hundreds of thousands of new companies are created and closed. Business is cutthroat, and no matter what you sell, there will always be competition in the market. It is up to you to find your niche and then master the art of negotiation and sales.

Ask yourself questions like: *What am I going to sell? How am I going to sell it? Who is my target customer? How much does it cost to start?* There are many more questions you could ask. Nonetheless, these simple questions are why it is important to study other business owners. By seeking advice from those who are doing what you want to do, you can learn from their processes, successes, and mistakes. This is also a way to figure out what you need to get started. Ask about estimated dollar amounts, certifications, licenses, and years of experience. Be courageous when you ask questions, as this is no different than questioning college students and graduates, current and former employees, or active and retired members of the military.

Also, know that an entrepreneur can have multiple streams of income that stem from their primary business. A cosmetologist could sell hairstyling services while also selling custom hair products. They could then create a tagline like "Extra Crispy" and print it on t-shirts for their customers to buy. They could also own a building and then rent booths out to other cosmetologists. Next, they could author a book for cosmetologists all around the world, teaching them how to grow their clientele. They could also perform workshops and private sessions to help cosmetologists in training. Be creative!

While reading this, someone may think, "I could also be an entrepreneur by illegally selling drugs." Yes, this is an option but a super risky one! Trust me when I tell you that it is much less stressful to choose legal options. Consider the wisdom of successful entrepreneur John Hope Bryant.

In an *Earn Your Leisure* interview entitled "Inside the Vault: How John Hope Bryant is Empowering a Nation with Financial Liberation", he acknowledges that *"drug dealers understand import, export, marketing, wholesale, retail, customer service, territory, and logistics."* However, he urges us to take his advice: *"A drug dealer or neighborhood hustler is not dumb, but they are making a dumb decision by choosing to stay in an illegal game that is rigged against us. Use the skills you have to do something legal!"* I hope this sticks with you.

E4: Enlistment

Joining the military is another viable option for students and graduates who are uncertain about what they want to do with their lives. This provides many benefits and opportunities to travel while meeting new people. However, be conscious of the freedom you are giving up for those benefits.

My father served 20 years in the military, and it came with essential aspects like housing, food, clothing, healthcare, discounts at certain stores, and special interest rates for cars, home loans, and insurance. Serving in the military allowed my father to meet my mother, as she also served. Although my father did not attend college, his service helped to pay for more than 90% of my college tuition. I also have friends who joined before, during, and after college to help pay for their tuition and loans.

A Combination of Es

Although I have given you the four options you have after high school, you do not have to choose only one. You can choose two, three, or all four! You could be a teacher during the day while also joining the National Guard Reserve. Added to that, you could be a virtual yoga instructor while taking online college classes to advance your career. That is just an example to spark thought. Try not to stretch yourself too thin.

The Journey of Deciding

Each of the options has its own pros and cons, as none of these options are all sunshine and rainbows. Many entrepreneurs face economic and emotional hardships; some college students regret their schools of choice; some members of the military miss their families and freedom; some employees dislike following directions from superiors. Take the necessary time to figure out what you want to do. Try new things, find your passion, and open your mind to the endless possibilities that you can find or create. Learn what is necessary. Then, take action. If you fail, learn from it, and try something different. Just because your ideal job, school, or business idea is not popular doesn't mean that it doesn't exist or that you cannot create it. It may even be on social media, but you just do not see it based on the accounts you follow. I am referring to the types of companies that make millions of dollars per year. They may not be popular, but they will always be needed.

We are all entrepreneurs, whether you own your own business or not. If you become an employee, you are an entrepreneur, and your employer is your largest client. Place emphasis on "largest," not "only." You can have a side hustle to increase your revenue streams and get paid for something that aligns with your passion. We are also multifaceted people. It is okay to express yourself in different areas while making money. You could have a six-figure salary as an engineer for Google but still love to do photography on the weekends for local weddings.

You can relate life to being in school, as you are given problems and then tasked with finding the solution. However, there are many ways to solve whatever problem you are faced with. In math class, I hated showing my work or writing out the process of how I got the answer. But now I see the reason why it was important to do so. By showing how I solved the problem, I can help others with their problems and even get rewarded for it. Do not let this analogy go over your head. **This is the road to riches, wealth, and internal satisfaction: earning income to help people solve problems to make their lives easier.**

You may still be asking yourself, "But how do I figure out what I want to do?" My advice is that you do this by visualizing and questioning what others do and by gaining experience in different jobs, roles, and industries. Most importantly, figure out what problems you are passionate about solving and then find a job that allows you to do so. You could also create a business. However, whether you choose to own your own business or not, you are still **the CEO of your life!** This means you are responsible for how disciplined and successful you are. I understand life and school can become overwhelming. Remain calm and take things one day at a time, while accomplishing one task at a time. From the book, *The ONE Thing* by Gary W. Keller and Jay Papasan, a great question to constantly ask yourself is *"What's the ONE Thing I can do, such that by doing it everything else will be easier or unnecessary?"*

Here is an excerpt from the book, *Rich & Righteous* by Jullien Gordon to further elaborate on the journey of deciding:

You are the cure to someone's cancer. It may not be the type of cancer you need chemotherapy for, but people have all types of cancers or problems in their life that you and your purpose are the solution to. Cancers come in many forms: financial, emotional, professional, mental, social, familial, nutritional, etc. You may solve problems for individuals or for organizations. Individuals experience problems at every level of Maslow's Hierarchy of Needs whether the need be physiological, safety, belonging and love, self-esteem, or self-actualization. And then organizations have problems in terms of marketing & sales, systems & processes, finance, and people. Pick your problem.

My Job Experiences

You may become an employee at 10 different companies before you figure out what you love to do. I held many different jobs in high school and college, and they all taught me something—whether it was skills, conversational talking points, or finding what I like and dislike. See the next page for a list of those jobs.

- **Neighborhood lawn care (independent work):** Time and energy are our number one commodities! I can only cut a certain amount of grass within a day for a low, fixed amount of money.
- **Kings Island:** While working in park admissions, I noticed how they mastered the thrill and entertainment industry, as well as the back-end logistics. I also saw the insane markup on food due to the scarcity of available options for visitors.
- **Sears:** I saw this retail company die slowly with a shortage of daily customers. I also got fired, which taught me the lesson that we are always being watched!
- **Xscape Theaters:** I learned that movie theaters make most of their money from concessions.
- **Furhaven Pet Products (warehouse factory):** I quickly realized that working on my feet all day was not for me! This was a seasonal job, and when the manager asked who wanted to be let go first, I gladly raised my hand.
- **Miami Business Summer Camp:** This camp demonstrated that most students are oblivious about college and life after high school. This was another spark in realizing how I could help those who followed in my footsteps.
- **KPMG (a corporate accounting firm):** I learned the power of networking, office politics, and how large companies utilize accounting. I thought this would be fun, but none of the positions piqued my interest.

Dear Kenny,

Along this life journey, there will be societal pressures saying that you must have every single detail of your future already figured out. But the truth is that life is an unpredictable journey. No life has ever existed that went exactly as they planned. Yes, it is important to plan and have goals, but know that the only constant is change. The people around you will change, your mindset will change, and your desires may change. Be flexible with this change, and do not place too much pressure on yourself to have every single detail of your future already figured out. When something does not happen in the exact sequence you envisioned, it can cause depression if you are being inflexible or placing too much pressure on yourself.

There is such thing as age or time pressure that makes us feel like we are behind or in constant competition. Society, family members, and peers who have been programmed to follow tradition will say things like: "By age 18, you should move out of the house. By age 25, you should have two college degrees and a job that pays you $60K a year. By 30, you should be married with two kids and owning your house." Whoa! Says who? Do not let these stereotypes, stigmas, or shackles control you! This is your life, and you are allowed to go at it at your own pace. I say this with caution because there are consequences to procrastinating on what you know you should be doing.

It is also important to be somewhat selfish with your time, money, and energy. We were taught that being selfish is always a bad thing. However, you must take care of yourself before you can take care of anyone else. An old saying often used to describe the important acts of self-care and self-preservation is "You cannot pour from an empty cup." You cannot give what you do not have, and you should not give more to others than what you give to yourself.

Sincerely,

Kenny Glenn, Success Coach and Entrepreneur

CHAPTER 4

My Personal Experience

Chapter 3 offers my advice to current high school students. Chapter 4 is about my personal experience. I am proud to be a graduate of Mt. Healthy High School in Cincinnati, Ohio. My father taught me this, as he proudly represents his alma mater of Withrow High School. This is the same for most other graduates from his school, as they are a tight-knit group that supports where they came from. They might literally bleed orange, which is their school color and motto! This strong foundational support is the vision I have for high schools around the nation, as students need to see more positive examples of those who look like them, especially those who walked the same streets and hallways as them.

When I was in high school, I only liked school for the social component, as I felt like sitting in most classes was meaningless. Thankfully, I was excellent at math and memorization. I could get an A on any test without studying. This allowed me to do my homework easily and quickly during school hours. Since I achieved honor roll every year, my grades were never an issue. My boredom in class led to my decision to be a class clown, and sometimes it would get me in trouble. During my 10th grade year, I had the option to attend trade school for my junior and senior years. I opted not to because of the incorrect but widely held stigma that students who chose to attend trade school would not go to college. Since my goal was to go to college, I decided to stay at my high school and attend regular classes. With the current high school system, if I had a choice, I would have only attended math and psychology classes. I would have spent the other hours working on my basketball skills because that is what I was most passionate about at the time.

The Love of Basketball

Thanks to my academic success, I already knew that college admission would not be a struggle. However, I still had the dream of receiving multiple athletic scholarship offers and becoming a Division I college athlete. This pushed me to shift most of my energy during non-school hours towards basketball. There was nothing I wanted more than to be on my school's basketball team. I mentioned earlier in the book that I got cut during basketball tryouts in both my freshman year AND my sophomore year. Not "Michael Jordan cut." He was not cut like me because he was placed on the junior varsity team. This meant he still got to represent his school in some way. But me, not at all. My type of cut after tryouts was where the coaches said something like, "Sorry, but we do not need you on our team. Try again next year."

From seventh grade to ninth grade, I ran on the cross-country team to keep busy, and I thought it would help with conditioning for basketball. Through the experience, I found out that I hated cross country and realized it did not help me become a better basketball player! Even with all the running, I still felt out of breath during my ninth-grade basketball tryouts. Now as I look back, I see how this inaccurate assumption and misinformation negatively affected me and still affects many athletes today.

Here, I offer important advice to athletes. Your training should be similar to how you will move in the sport you are training for. In a football, basketball, or soccer game, you are not running nonstop like in a cross-country race or a mile-long run. Instead, multiple short bursts of speed with lateral movements are involved.

When my tenth-grade year came around, I tried out for the team again, and I got cut AGAIN! The coaches posted the names of the students they chose to be on the final rosters and my name was nowhere to be found. I took a picture of that list and furiously vowed that I would never get cut again. During tryouts, I noticed how I would guarantee myself a spot on the team next year. I knew that if I could dunk, there was no way they would reject me. Basketball coaches know that jumping ability brings more than just dunking, as it also brings the tangible aspects of rebounding and shot blocking.

After getting cut, I learned of a local basketball organization called the Hilltop Hawks. This was a league composed of other local high school students who loved basketball but did not make their high school teams. Regardless of who the competition was, this was an opportunity to play the game I loved while enhancing my skills. However, if you would have watched me play outside of tryouts, you would have wondered, "How in the world did this kid not make his high school basketball team!?"

When I played pickup games at the local YMCA, I would be one of the best players on the court, regardless of who was there. This included fully grown men and local high school players. **One word: confidence.** When tryouts came around, I would be too nervous and worried about being perfect in front of the coaches and my classmates. I was afraid of missing shots or getting the ball stolen. However, this was not the case any other time, such as when I would play my father one on one. I would try to

47

demolish my father every time we played one on one because that is what every son dreams of: eventually beating his father at anything! He eventually taught me the important lesson of always playing with the same confidence and ferocity that I had when I played against him, no matter who was watching.

Dear Kenny,

I attribute all my successes to finally being CONFIDENT in myself and my training. I realized that it does not matter what others think of me, nor should I cloud my headspace by trying to read people's minds. All that matters is that you do what you have already practiced. You might have fearful thoughts such as:

"What if I miss?"

"What if I commit a turnover?"

"What if my team loses?"

These thoughts may go through your head, but you must know that the opposite is also true! What if you make the shot? What if everything goes perfectly? There is only one way to find out, and every shot you do not take is an automatic miss. When the lights are on and everyone is watching, do the same things you do when no one is there.

Sincerely,

Kenny Glenn, Success Coach and Entrepreneur

Here are three monumental moments that I vividly remember about my process to achieve my goals to dunk and make the basketball team in my 11th-grade year:

1. One night while leaving a local YMCA basketball court, my father told me to touch the rim. On my first attempt, I did more than just touch it, I was able to grab it! Once I accomplished that feat, I knew I was on the right path

towards dunking. Next, I began doing 1,000 calf raises per day, studying NBA workout tips from magazines, doing plyometrics in the street, and a prison-style squat workout that would burn my legs so much that I could barely walk afterwards. With a few more weeks of intense training, on December 20, 2011, at 14 years young, I dunked for the first time! My dad was there to witness it, and I could not stop smiling the entire day!

2. In the 10th grade, after basketball season ended, I asked my teacher for a bathroom pass, but truthfully, I went to go meet with Coach Clark, the varsity basketball coach. Since Coach Clark was also a math teacher at our school, it was easy to access him. I wanted to speak with him to learn what I could do to ensure a spot on next year's team. Unfortunately, he was not in his room. Instead of just walking out, I decided to write him a message on a sticky note. It expressed my passion, mentioned my dunking ability, and included my cell phone number. I returned to class, and 10 minutes later, I received a text message from Coach Clark telling me to come to his room ASAP. I do not remember if I asked to go to the bathroom again or if I just walked out, but at that moment, I did not fear any consequences because I knew how important this meeting would be and how badly I wanted to be on the team. During our meeting, Coach Clark noticed my growth spurt and he told me that I could accompany the team for scrimmages at local high schools and summer open gyms. I was already practicing at the YMCA every day, but this was a major step towards achieving my goal!

3. On the last day of my 10th-grade year, we had a scheduled school-wide pep rally to celebrate the academic year. Since I was so intently focused on basketball, in my mind

there was nothing to celebrate. I told my neighbor and brother, Joseph Abrams, that instead of going to the pep rally, I would much rather use the extra time to go play basketball. He agreed to come with me if I chose to do so. Next, I sent my mother a text asking if she could come to pick us up from school and take us to the YMCA. That entire summer, I took every opportunity to be at the YMCA or any basketball court to improve my strength and skills. I would ride my bike on streets that had no sidewalks or get dropped off with no confirmed ride back home. I was so determined that I would be there all day with only a couple of dollars for vending machine snacks. One day in the gym, I told Joseph that "jaws are going to drop next season." I knew that our classmates and coaches were not going to believe how much better I had become. Nor would they be able to fathom my new level of confidence or my jumping ability.

Dear Kenny,

Before you can be truly great at anything, you must do it over and over and over again. It is as simple as that. Repetition is what builds muscle memory, mental fortitude, and confidence. Can you pour a cup of water? How do you know? Because you have done it thousands of times. It does not matter if you had to pour a cup of water in your house at midnight or in the middle of a graduation ceremony with thousands of people staring at you.

Use my story as an example to increase your focus and determination to achieve whatever you truly desire. Have confidence and the guts to do what it takes! The time is going to pass anyway. You might as well use it to your benefit.

Sincerely,

Kenny Glenn, Success Coach and Entrepreneur

My 11th-grade year came around, and of course, I made the basketball team because I had practiced with them during the summer. That was when I noticed that varsity tryouts were a joke. The coaches already knew who the real hoopers were, and the only way someone else was going to make the team is if they unexpectedly stood out and made a major impact. When the season began, fear and nervousness crept into my mind again. Transitioning from the Hilltop league and YMCA pick-up games to high school varsity games with referees and roaring crowds was not easy. Now the whole school was coming to see me play, and it felt like the game was moving lightning fast! There were many times when I was afraid of making a mistake that would lead to my coach taking me out of the game. I would also worry about what my classmates in the stands would think and if they would laugh at me. Even though I was nervous and did not get much playing time, I still leveraged my strengths. I used my athleticism and jumping ability to get steals, grab rebounds, and make easy putback layups.

Dear Kenny,

Once I made the basketball team, everyone at school knew my name, and certain girls started to give me more attention. Funny thing is, they were the same girls that I tried to talk to before achieving a spot on the basketball team. They rejected my attention until others started to give it to me. I used to be upset at this reality, but now I realize that it is just human nature. BUT! ... Even with this new fame and attention, remember to stay focused on your goals. Attention is an inevitable byproduct of the work that you put in. Be great and be grateful. Be great by repeatedly giving everyone positive reasons to keep watching you. Knowing that you can lose it all in the blink of an eye, be grateful.

Sincerely,

Kenny Glenn, Success Coach and Entrepreneur

I mentioned in the failure section of the introduction that I embarrassingly missed my first in-game dunk attempt during my junior year. This occurred on my home court on my father's birthday while he was watching in the stands. In this specific game, I got the most playing time I had ever gotten! Before I missed, I was exhausted, and I signaled to Coach Clark to substitute me ASAP. Right before my replacement was coming, I got a steal and a wide-open fast break! I could have easily done a lay-up, but I felt like I had to try to dunk! This was the most nervous moment of my life which might be why it felt like my legs gave out. LOL! The lesson here is you can bounce back from anything. I had already been cut twice so nothing could be more embarrassing, and I knew I would have more chances to dunk.

After my junior year season in school, I played a season of AAU basketball with a team called the Cincinnati Rockerz. I thank Coach Milan Lanier, Coach Matt Birch, and Coach Paul Miller for the opportunity! I also thank my parents for paying for it. This experience helped to increase the level of confidence that I would need during my senior year of high school. AAU offered the opportunity to travel and play all around the country against high-level competition. We were playing at least three games every weekend which catapulted my experience and made the game easier. Thanks to the fact that my AAU team had some of my high school teammates, it grew our bond and chemistry on and off the court. Shoutout to Milan Lanier Jr., Brandon Birch, Kenneth English, Hjavier Pitts, Kylan Miller, and Germaine Britten.

Of course, I continued to practice my skills after the AAU basketball season. Going into my senior season, I displayed my heightened skills during pickup games and scrimmages against local high schools. Sadly, right before the season, a tragedy left my high school community's collective heart broken. A graduate of my high school, three-sport standout athlete, hilarious guy, and a person who was like by all, was killed. His name is Vince Turnage Jr., and his impact will live forever. Vince died on a Sunday, and he had just visited our basketball practice two days earlier. We talked about playing against each other. Many of my classmates and I looked up to Vince because he was great at everything he did and made it look effortless. This tragedy forced me to realize how fragile life is.

As the first game of senior year approached, my father told me, "Don't wait until the last game of the season to show them how great you are." I used his advice to be much more vocal and dominant than I was during my junior year. The other major differences were that I was a starter and that I confidently shot and dunked the ball in almost every game.

Then, unexpectedly, at the end of a game later in the season, I got elbowed in the eye and it almost ended my high school career. The hit caused me to constantly have double vision. I went to three different doctors and each of them diagnosed an orbital floor fracture that would require surgery. I sobbed like a baby when I heard this news because it would have meant everything I worked for was over with. Thankfully, my parents gave me the option to choose if I would have the surgery or not. I chose to not have the surgery, and eventually, my eye completely healed. I thank God and all my ancestors for this miracle! I was able to finish with my teammates, and we had lots of fun while we won most of our games.

Dear Kenny,

Fear of failure and fear of criticism are what stop most people from achieving their goals and being their true selves. NO ONE IS PERFECT AT EVERYTHING THEY DO! Even if it seems as if they are perfect, they had to work and fail so they could achieve what looks like perfection. I will use Kobe Bryant for example. He is a Naismith Memorial Basketball Hall of Famer who won five NBA championships, and he is the fourth-highest scorer of all time in the NBA. But guess what, he has also missed more shots than any-one else. Regardless of the result, he kept on shooting his way to becoming one of the greatest basketball players ever. The lesson here is to "shoot your shot"! Go after that goal, talk to that person to whom you are attracted, apply to that job or college, and move to a new city or state. The worst that could happen is that you get rejected. No one likes rejection, but it is a part of life and something that everyone experiences. Be thankful for every "no," every rejection, and every failed attempt. I promise you will learn from each of them. I understand that you may be afraid, but this is where courage is necessary. Courage is the act of doing something even though you are afraid.

The most famous quote from Dr. Eric Thomas, aka the Hip-Hop Preacher, is "When you want to succeed as bad as you want to breathe, then you'll be successful!" When I got cut from the basketball team for the second time, I listened to this specific YouTube video every single day while I worked to make sure I never got cut again! When you truly want something, you can't just kind of want it or give half of your effort.

Sincerely,

Kenny Glenn, Success Coach and Entrepreneur

College Student?

In this section, I will explain my pursuit of becoming a college student, whether I would become a college athlete or not. After graduating high school in 2014, I knew that the best choice for me, with or without athletics, was to attend college. Growing up, I saw that those around me who were celebrated by others and seemed to be enjoying life to the fullest either were in college or had graduated from college.

One day, my mother straight up told me that she and my father could not afford to fully pay for my college aspirations. This is when I realized that I was completely unaware of the reality of economics and our family's financial standing. It was my perception that we had enough money to pay for anything. I saw my parents go to work every day, we ate three meals with snacks, all the bills were paid, and we owned four cars. My mother then explained to me the importance of scholarships and how the college I chose would be a financial decision. The money I received to attend certain schools would depend on my GPA, my ACT score, my admission essay, and the collective finances of my parents. My GPA was 3.8, but after three attempts, my highest ACT score was only 22. That score was fine by me because I struggled with that test due to the pressure associated with it, along with sitting in a classroom for half of the day.

Dear Kenny,

It is important that a student knows as early as middle school about the finances of their household. Understand that a salary or hourly wage is just the top. Take into consideration that they must pay bills and taxes. Then, whatever money is left will pay for food, transportation, vacations, education, amusement, and entertainment. With this understanding, you will now be able to broaden your view of the world and the financial responsibilities of maintaining a household. This information will help you determine what type of lifestyle you want to eventually live.

Sincerely,

Kenny Glenn, Success Coach and Entrepreneur

My mother took me to a college fair she heard about on the radio. This was an event where hundreds of colleges had booths with information about their institution, along with free items. The information they asked for was my name, my high school, and my address. After this fair, I started to receive dozens of letters of mail from colleges all over the country that wanted me to apply.

My first academic choice was to attend the University of Miami in Florida because of the nonstop sunshine and access to the beach. They also had a great basketball team that I wanted to be a part of. My mother and I went to an information session for this school, and my dreams were hilariously crushed. Their average ACT score was between 28 and 32, compared to my 22. Plus, they were a private institution, meaning the tuition would be much higher than a public institution. We left soon after we heard these points, and I knew it was time to switch my focus to other schools. Two other important factors led me to narrow my options for where to apply. My father's military involvement allowed 90% of my tuition to be paid for, but the caveat was that I had to choose a school in Ohio. Furthermore, out-of-state public colleges typically charged double the amount of in-state tuition.

I applied & was accepted by the University of Cincinnati, Miami University, The Ohio State University, and Xavier University. Around this same time, I was awarded a plaque and scholarship from Honda and The Ohio State University for being the best math student at my school. This was a great achievement, but I chose not to go to The Ohio State University due to its massive size and student population. Xavier University offered me a scholarship for $17,000 per year! That sounded great until I learned they were a private institution with a hefty tuition price tag of $34,000 per year. After learning that, I crossed them off the list, too.

Although I had good grades, I was also lazy and did not want to write multiple essays that scholarship applications asked for. Thankfully, my GPA granted me automatic scholarships from the colleges I applied to. I was also awarded scholarships from my high school. Miami University then invited me to an event called The Bridges Program with a $20,000 scholarship tied to it. In 2013, this program invited high-achieving high school seniors from historically underrepresented demographics to engage with current students, faculty, and staff. The program allowed us to meet students from Cincinnati, Dayton, Columbus, and Cleveland. We were taken on tours of the facilities, and we spent the night in residence halls with current Miami students. Miami University also invited me and two friends to a basketball game for free! At this event, we were informed of the different options of majors we could choose from. The campus was beautiful, everyone seemed friendly, and the Bridges program gave me the perception that I would be in classes with students who looked like me. I was sold, and knew I wanted to attend Miami University! However, it would have cost $10,000 more than attending the University of Cincinnati because of room and board.

On May 1 of my senior year, which was National College Decision Day, I felt pressured to officially choose which college I would attend. I chose the University of Cincinnati since it was close to home, and I had already established a relationship with the Black faculty in the engineering department. My plan was to enjoy my entire summer by training at the gym so I could try out for the University of Cincinnati basketball team as a walk-on. Although I tried to hide it from her, my mother found out that I had an opportunity to start college early by attending a six-week program that included a dorm room, a scholarship, and classes I would receive credit for.

College Athlete?

I will get into the details of my story later, in the Hall of Fame chapter, but now I will explain everything I did before and during my senior year of high school to become a college athlete.

Dear Kenny,

Obtaining a college athletic scholarship is simple and just like getting anything else in life. However, "simple" does not mean "easy." If you truly want something, you must GO GET IT! Be creative and be willing to give whatever it takes. Are you merely interested in getting what you want, or are you committed?

Sincerely, Kenny Glenn, Success Coach and Entrepreneur

My first attempt at gaining an athletic scholarship was emailing prep school and college basketball coaches. I even used Instagram to direct-message an NBA player to learn how he transitioned from a local high school to a nationally-ranked prep school. I considered prep school because it would give me more time to mature. However, prep schools that allowed high school graduates to still showcase their talent without impacting their college eligibility were not as popular as they are now. This, coupled with my academic success made college the more obvious choice. I did not receive many email replies, but an assistant coach from FAMU did reply. He advised me to continue to work on my game and then go to prep school due to my young age and varsity experience. Even with all the work I put in and the great senior season I had, I did not have the type of statistics or popularity that would bring me attention or scholarship offers from coaches.

After the season, my father accompanied my teammate Andrew Wilfong and me on a visit to Miami University – Hamilton Campus to speak with the coach about playing college basketball. No offense to anyone who chooses to play in the United States Collegiate Athletic Association (USCAA), but Wilfong and I knew that we were much greater athletes than what this campus had to offer. After the visit, I figured I would just choose a college at the NCAA Division I level where my academics would get me accepted, and then, I would try to join its basketball team as a walk-on. As I stated in the previous section, the original plan was to do this at the University of Cincinnati.

Next, I shifted my mind to what most other male high school students were thinking about: graduation, girls, and taking advantage of my new driver's license. With my license also came my mother's former car, a 2005 Honda Accord. That was my baby! At least it was until my college teammate crashed into me and totaled it...but that is another story. In order to have money to put gas in the car, I had to find a job. I became a cashier at Sears. I also wanted to use that money to go on dates with my girlfriend.

Around this same time, I considered running track because the head coach, Ken Meibers, noticed my jumping ability and asked me to come high jump. During my ninth-grade year, I performed the high jump for two meets but soon quit the team because I was terrible. But as I explained earlier, my insane work ethic completely changed that. With these thoughts in my head, I told my mom I was considering not doing track so I could focus on making money. This is an example of the short-term thinking that teenagers and even some adults have. Thankfully, my mother is a wise woman who thinks both short-term and long-term. She explained that since it was my senior year, I had nothing to lose and everything to gain by competing in track. She also pointed out that I had my whole life to work a job, but high school was coming to an end soon. Her words made sense. So, I opted to listen to her advice by staying on the track team while keeping my job but working less.

After school, I would drive to track practice. Then, some days after practice, I would drive to work. The original plan was to only compete in the high jump, but then, I became attracted to the long jump because of the sand. At each track meet, I either won or placed in the top three in both of my events. Even with this success, my heart was still tied to basketball, and I did not see a real future in track & field. However, during the regional track meet, which is the last meet before the state championships, I gained unsolicited attention from a college coach: Jeff Hill, the coach at Thomas More University in Crestview Hills, Kentucky. Coach Hill was also an alum of my high school, and he held the long jump record I was trying to beat!

Here is a funny but meaningful story about that specific track meet. This meet spanned two days: Tuesday and Thursday. On Tuesday, I qualified for the long jump. The high jump was scheduled for Thursday. When I arrived at the track on Thursday, I realized that I had lost my spikes! I found the janitor and told him what they looked like, and he allowed me to search for them in the lost and found. I could not find them, but I did see a different pair of jump spikes that were exactly my size. I told my teammate, David Montgomery, who is now the star NFL running back for the Chicago Bears, what the spikes looked like and what to tell the janitor. He did exactly what I told him and got the spikes for me to compete in! Thanks Dave!

However, even after getting the spikes, I called my father and told him that since I had already qualified for State in the long jump, I was contemplating not doing the high jump. His wise response was: "You did not come this far just to quit." My dad was right! This would not be the last time where I wanted to stop and he encouraged me to keep going. I gave it my all, and I qualified for the last spot! The person I beat was the quarterback of the football team that won the most recent state championship. He and his team beat my classmates. So this was my way of getting some type of competitive revenge for them.

It was a major accomplishment to qualify for the state meet, especially in two events. This created even more exposure for my pursuit to become a college athlete. I would be competing against the best competition in the state at The Ohio State University in Columbus, Ohio. Before my long jump competition, my father said these powerful words: "No matter what, we are proud of you." I almost shed tears when I heard that, but I knew it was time to show why I deserved to be there!

In the long jump, I won sixth place, and in the high jump, I won eighth place. This was pretty good for a kid who only took track seriously during his senior year of high school. In the Hall of Fame chapter, I will explain what happened after the state meet that led to me truly becoming a college athlete. After the state meet, I attracted more attention from different college coaches. Thanks to my constant communication with Coach Jeff Hill, he scheduled me to physically visit the campus of Thomas More University. My mother went with me, but similar to my visit to the Hamilton branch campus of Miami University, I knew I was a better athlete than what they had to offer. Their campus was small, and athletically, they were an NAIA school, which was much lower than my aspirations of competing at the NCAA Division I level.

On the same day, I texted the Miami University track coach, Chad Reynolds, as it was the last day that recruits were allowed to be in contact with college coaches. Coach Reynolds invited me to come meet him in person and tour the athletic facilities. My mother saw my joy and agreed to drive an hour to visit Miami University with me. I was amazed by the facilities and how much Coach Reynolds believed that I could be a benefit to the track team. He offered me a guaranteed spot and said he would do everything in his power to reinstate my academic scholarships, even though the deadline to accept them had passed. He also told me that the team did not have any athletic scholarship money left to give that year, but he assured me that I would have the opportunity to earn a scholarship the following year. I was super hype but still needed time to think and talk it over with my parents.

Nevertheless, a week after my athletic visits, my parents dropped me off at the University of Cincinnati (UC) to begin the early college program that I originally attempted to avoid. Just like in junior high school, I did not want to go because I believed in my athletic abilities. At least, attending this program allowed me to reconnect with some of the students I met during my previous summer programs. Added to that list of students, I met Annette Echikunwoke, who is now an NCAA Champion and an Olympian! Annette kindly gave me the contact information for her coach so I could speak with him about joining their team.

After being on campus for a week, I met with the UC track coach and explained my young age, track events, personal best marks, and high school success. These aspects did not entice him enough to offer me a spot. Instead, he told me that I would have to try out for the team as a walk-on, without any formal coaching. My decision was crystal clear after this. The next day, I called my parents and told them that I was going to Miami, the place where I was needed and wanted! I believed in myself and so did Coach Chad Reynolds. I informed the UC program directors of my decision to leave, and then my parents came to pick me up. People still ask me why I did not run track at UC, and this is the exact reason. Fast forward, and now, I am a record-holding, national-qualifying, gold medal-winning professional athlete with no college debt!

Dear Kenny,

There are situations when listening to your parents makes dollars and sense. I have achieved and experienced so many great things because of my parents' advice and guidance to give my all in the classroom and in sports. This led to me keeping a high GPA and focusing on the long-term benefits of excelling in track & field instead of working too many hours at a job. I sacrificed the short-term money ($800 checks) to get the long-term money (college scholarships worth $80,000).GPA equals dollars! Your GPA is comparable to a credit score as it determines how much money you can earn to pay for college and even put directly into your bank account. Think about it like this. Would a college or scholarship committee rather give $20,000 to a student with a 3.8 GPA or a student with a 2.8 GPA? Yes, there are other factors, but your GPA carries the most weight.

Believe in yourself, no matter your age! I was 16 during the entire journey of becoming a college athlete. My parents did not agree with every decision I made. Yet, they still supported me because they saw my passion and ability to figure anything out.

Sincerely,

Kenny Glenn, Success Coach and Entrepreneur

CHAPTER 5

The System

I am pro-options and pro-education, but this is different from simply being pro-school and gaining general knowledge just for acquisition's sake. We have been told that education and school are the same thing, but they are not. School has an end, but education is infinite. In his famous book, *Think & Grow Rich*, Napoleon Hill explains why knowledge alone does not equate to power:

Knowledge will not attract money, unless it is organized, and intelligently directed, through practical *plans of action*, to the *definite end* of accumulation of money. Lack of understanding of this fact has been the source of confusion to millions of people who falsely believe that "knowledge is power." (Page 73)

In the same book, Napoleon Hill then breaks down the original meaning of the word "education."

That word (education) is derived from the Latin word "educo," meaning to educe, to draw out, to *develop from within*. An educated man is not, necessarily, one who has an abundance of general or specialized knowledge. An educated man is one who has so developed the faculties of his mind that he may acquire anything he wants, or its equivalent, without violating the rights of others. (Page 73)

Students and graduates should seek specialized knowledge and then find creative ways to leverage it to get what they want and to achieve their definitions of success. This is how people truly become educated, whether they utilize school or not. You must tap into and unleash the power of your mind! School is a viable option but only if you understand the true meaning of education. College is not for everyone, but it is my opinion that everyone should at least give themselves the option of attending college.

When I use the word "success," I am referring to mental, physical, spiritual, and financial well-being. You must define success for yourself and not limit it to a job or salary. No type of schooling will guarantee success, but **you can obtain your desired job or salary and much more by properly leveraging school, expanding your network, gaining meaningful experiences, and fine-tuning your ability to properly market yourself.**

In theory, we go to school to learn, but what are we really learning? Students often ask, "When will I use this?" or "Why do I need to know that?" In school, I was placed in math classes but not taught how to apply math towards personal financial literacy or decision making. I was placed in science classes such as biology and chemistry but not taught about how they relate to the foods we should eat for healthy lives. I was placed in English classes, but I was not taught how to effectively or properly communicate in personal or professional settings. I was placed in history classes, but although I am a student of African descent, I was not taught about Afrocentricity. Due to this reality and other reasons, school tends to serve as a conveyer belt for future miserable employees because it lacks a transferable connection to the world after high school.

I entered college not knowing how to properly write an email or a resume. I was not taught these aspects of formal writing until I was a junior in college taking an introductory business course. I still remember a terrible email that I sent to my calculus professor during my first semester of college. It read along the lines of: "Yo, why is my grade not updated?" That is no way to address a professor, but I did not know any better. In high school, if I found discrepancies, I would just wait until I saw these teachers again since we saw each other every day. However, this is not the case in college. There are days in between classes that delay opportunities to speak with professors face to face.

No school, at any grade or level, intentionally taught me about sales. But in my opinion, the ability to sell is the best educational tool to have. Have you ever noticed that colleges have all kinds of majors and specializations except in the subject of sales? I learned sales from selling candy as a kid, selling my skills in job interviews, and selling my potential to attract women. I learned how to articulate myself as the optimal choice in a nonharmful manner and without being deceitful. We all know people and companies who lie and trick others to get what they want. That style of sales just does not sit right with my spirit. I would rather someone reject, dislike, or hate me for telling the truth than for them to love me based on fairytale lies that make them feel good.

In 2021, the State of Ohio passed a law that makes it mandatory for high schools to teach at least one semester of financial literacy. If taught correctly, this is arguably the most important class that a high school student will take from a life skills perspective. Finances govern most of our decisions. Note that it is the number one reason for crime and divorce. Every day and almost every hour, we ask: "How much does it cost? What am I going to eat? Where am I going to live? What am I going to wear? Whose Netflix account can I use for free?" In America, the financial topics of risk/reward ratio, cost-benefit analysis, budgeting, credit, investing, cost of living, and taxes are inescapable. Therefore, it would make sense to learn them at least on a basic level.

Mathematics

When I ask students about their grades, they will typically say that their worst grade is in math class. When I ask why they struggle, they say it is due to not seeing the importance of the subject beyond the basics, or they just are not good at it, which causes them not to try. The subject of math should be taken more seriously and taught in a way that is relatable to the students. With students and family members who struggle, I can teach and explain, in a simple manner, various concepts and problems that seem complex at first. I do this by rephrasing questions. I once wondered about the importance of a high-level course like calculus. It was not until I took it for the second time that I understood calculus was more about critical thinking and bringing together every level of mathematics to solve problems.

We live in a universe that revolves around mathematics. Individuals who lead the masses tend to be mathematical thinkers who can break things down in their minds and find solutions. Let us look at this example. If someone were to give you a 600-page book that has the potential to change your life if you read it, that number 600 may seem like too big of a pill to swallow. Just break it down; 600 pages divided by 30 days is only 20 pages per day for a month. Another option is to spread it out over 60 days, which is only 10 pages a day. If you have time to watch TV, be on social media, or go to parties, then you have time to accomplish tasks that will positively benefit your future. It is mathematical to have the ability to break things down, know what to do, and then execute the plan to arrive at the correct solution.

Digital Pros and Cons

For most people, wrapped all into one, cell phones have become the most preferred sources of information, communication, and dopamine hits. We depend on our phones as our alarm clock, our newspaper, our photo album, our GPS, our game system, and more. Once upon a time, we depended on radio and television broadcasts or printed books that required us to go inside physical buildings to retrieve information. We had one phone or large computer per household. More often than not, we had to wait at least one week before packages would ship to our homes. These realities forced us to exercise gratitude, patience, and dependency, even at the expense of remaining somewhat ignorant. We also did not spend hours staring at a tiny screen, constantly receiving rushes of dopamine from messages, likes, comments, buzzes, and pings. Our devices have become our biggest addiction and have made it much easier to fall victim to the overconsumption of our vices. Notice how far we have come as a society, as now we can have what we need and want with much greater convenience. This new digital and automated world has brought great advantages but not without some harmful effects.

With cell phones as our new teachers, content posted on social media platforms and streaming services has turned into the new lesson plan. Both have captured the minds and attention of our society, regardless of age. Social media has made the world smaller, and we can access anyone across the globe who uses it. Although content can serve as a benefit, most consumers become drenched by overwhelming distractions. There are so many social media platforms and streaming services, and we are expected to be on and participate in each one of them. Society and our peers induce FOMO (fear of missing out) in us if we choose not to participate. However, by trying to see everything that is posted or released, our dreams and goals get pushed further and further away. DISTRACTions take us further away from what we seek to ATTRACT.

I make sure I use the available content for my benefit to help me learn and get closer to my goals. I advise everyone to do their best to follow suit. Sadly, too many people procrastinate or search for instant gratification by spending an insane amount of their days scrolling and posting on social media or binge-watching movies and shows. Something I have often done to mitigate these distractions is deleting social media apps from my phone for consecutive months. Deleting the apps eliminated my urge to scroll, which helped me to focus on achieving my goals in the classroom and in my sport. I replaced the time I would spend on social media with studying for class or watching sports films.

Here are **the four Es of content** that you should be conscious of.

1. **Educate:** learning applicable information on how to better yourself, your situation, or accomplish tasks and goals
2. **Entertain:** laughing at funny movies, memes, and short videos
3. **Eroticize:** sexually fantasizing over porn or half-naked photos and videos
4. **Escape:** mindlessly scrolling to pass time or procrastinate

When I decide to consume content or use social media, it is mostly for learning beneficial and applicable information. I also use it to connect with experts in different fields like mindset strengthening, athletics, finances, and nutrition. I then find or create opportunities to meet these specific expert groups or individuals in person. Experts whom I never would have met without social media include Lance Kearse, Derick Grant, and Sumair Bhasin. Fortunately, I discovered their Instagram pages. The original intent of social media remains, as we still use it to see what our friends and family are doing. However, we must know that most people only post their wins or what they think people want to see. As much as I try to stay focused, because I follow friends and family, distractions and gossip still pop up.

Here I offer some more personal tips and examples of how to leverage social media for your benefit:

- Establish a bio that quickly tells who you are, and post content that resembles that. Now, when you message people, you want to learn from or speak with, whatever you are saying or asking for will be easier to get across.
- Turn off social media notifications. The constant sounds, vibrations, and updates will lower your focus and affect your dopamine receptors. Otherwise, you can become addicted to social media and continually depend on it for your happiness.
- Reach out to the experts! During my sophomore year of college, I used Instagram to direct message multiple long jumpers. Some of them were Olympians like Mike Hartfield and Marquis Dendy. They replied to me and gave great advice on how I could improve! When I recognize gaps in my knowledge that can be filled with useful information, it makes sense to seek guidance from those who have been where I have been and who are currently doing, or have done, what I am seeking to accomplish.

Dear Kenny,

Do not get wrapped up in the social media matrix. Use it to learn, laugh, and stay in contact with people you meet along your journey. But beware of the negatives that it can induce. It can be the thief of joy! Likes, followers, comments, retweets, and reposts do not determine your self-worth. Some people and companies literally buy likes and followers. So it isn't even a fair metric. Remain true to yourself and remember there is an entire universe outside of social media.

I want you to also understand the power that imagery has on your mind. Social media is full of images that can sway your thinking. This is how some people can persuade you into living a false reality. Always remain skeptical and know that your mind is a garden that should be properly seeded and carefully tended to. There will also be weeds that you should remove from your garden.

Bob Proctor said it best: "If you can see it in your mind, you can hold it in your hand." This can refer to dreams and goals, material items, or people.

Seeing something in your mind before you hold it in your hand occurs by using your imagination. Allow me to break down the word "imagination" even further. Image-Nation... your mind, operates as a nation of images. This is why pictures "are worth a thousand words," why "seeing is believing," and why people say, "I knew and saw this happen before it truly did."

Do you "see" what I'm saying?

Sincerely,

Kenny Glenn, Success Coach and Entrepreneur

Meditation and Metacognition

When we are constantly distracted by noises and notifications, it eats at our time and limits our ability to focus. Think about what most people do on a typical day. We constantly consume information and food, and we complete various tasks. Where is the time to be at peace and truly think about our thoughts? Many students are unaware of meditation and the benefits it brings because they are not taught about it. When we hear the word meditation, we have been programmed to think of a monk figure humming and sitting with crossed legs. However, anything that brings you peace and some type of quietness or stillness can be classified as meditation. Meditation is the reason many people have their best ideas in the shower. In this scenario, we are alone and allowed to think in peace. Thankfully, there are other ways to do this besides showering and increasing your water bill. In doing so, I recommend that every reader remove themselves from other people or any technological distractions for at least five minutes a day. This will give you the opportunity to reflect and focus on your breath. Alone time also helps with accomplishing tasks that take longer than they should due to the distractions that come from other people and sources of entertainment.

Time to meditate allows for the process of metacognition to occur. Metacognition is the process of thinking about what you are thinking about. Within this process, you are questioning yourself and the thoughts that pop up in your mind. You evaluate what you allow to occupy your mind. Think about the benefits this could have on students if they were taught how to implement this concept. Metacognition allows us to respond to situations based on logic instead of reacting too quickly or automatically based on emotions. This would certainly help people, including students, to stay out of unnecessary trouble.

For example, a student in class questions their thoughts and has a conversation in their mind before making a decision: "If I talk when I am not supposed to, I might get in trouble or kicked out of class. What will happen then? That would lead to me becoming upset or missing assignments and key information for our upcoming exam. It will lower my grade and my chances of getting certain scholarships... Maybe I should just keep quiet."

Change the System?

The modern version of the school system operates as it was designed to; however, there are obvious needs for change as the world has changed and continues to do so. We must implement new methods and curricula that fuse academia with the diverse cultural backgrounds and interests of students. This also includes the dire need for integrating the five core competencies of social-emotional learning: self-awareness, self-management, social awareness, responsible decision making, and relationship skills.

Today's students and graduates are more stressed-out than ever before due to, but not limited to, family and financial pressures, unhealthy comparisons, and unrealistic expectations. Regardless of how long it takes to change a system that may seem to inevitably remain the same, we must take the power into our own hands. As I alluded to earlier in this chapter and on the back cover of this book, school and education are not the same thing. An educated person knows how to acquire anything they want by using the power of their mind and the resources around them. A person who overly depends on what they are taught in the confines of school only knows how to follow directions and regurgitate information. Students must recognize the power within themselves and their technological devices. Then use both to learn applicable information and connect with mentors.

Dear Kenny,

Be rebellious, leverage school, and seek true education.

Sincerely,

Kenny Glenn, Success Coach and Entrepreneur

Learn How to Learn

During an interview on the Breakfast Club radio show, 19 Keys gave some amazing points in terms of education. I have included a snippet of those powerful words, followed by my own synopsis:

> "With the proper mindset, you can learn any skill set. The first thing we must do is learn how to learn. We live in a time where information is so accessible that we do not value it, nor do we know how to decipher facts from fiction."

Some of us developed lackluster learning habits that stem from our parents and the current school system. How often have you or someone you know gotten upset when attempting to learn something new? It is my opinion that we should find ways that are best for us to digest information and make it relatable. Even if the content is difficult at first, we have the ability to creatively break it down in a way for us to understand it.

Many of us, and even myself, will blame the school system for what they did not teach us. That blame and potential anger does have merit, but some of the missing information is a blessing. But how? If someone or something taught you everything you needed to know, it would limit your ability to go and figure things out on your own.

SECTION 3: LEGACY

Plan to leave something behind so your name will live on.
No matter what, the game lives on.

— NAS

CHAPTER 6

The Hall of Fame

This chapter encompasses multiple aspects of greatness. I explain the moment I initiated my passion and impacted the lives of notable alumni while also setting and achieving a goal that would cement my legacy. When we hear or read the term "Hall of Fame," most of us only think about athletics. However, I want to impose a new thought, the Mental Hall of Fame. This is composed of individuals or groups who have inspired you and provided the necessary spark or guidance to improve your life. I am proud to say that I am a member of my high school's athletic and mental halls of fame.

> **"Set a bar for yourself, and then go over it."**
> I wrote this during my senior year of high school as a caption for an Instagram post of me flying over a high jump bar.

On October 14, 2016, I went back to my high school to speak to a senior class of student-athletes. This class was taught by Ms. Lori Miller, a high school teacher of mine for Accounting and Sports Management. Ms. Miller eventually became an Athletic Director and one of the key teachers who wrote me a letter of recommendation and allowed me to use the school's fitness equipment after I graduated. On this occasion, she gave me the opportunity to speak about life after high school. This was my chance to give advice to the younger versions of myself by letting them know the possibilities of achieving their dreams, despite the many negative temptations that would pull at them.

Even with a fear of public speaking, I became the very thing that my peers and I did not have when we were in school. We did not have alumni who intentionally came back to give transparent advice about their journeys. As students, it would have been highly beneficial to hear from alumni who were doing the exact things we dreamed about as students. At the time of my speech, I was 19 years young, a third-year student at a prestigious college, and a top-ranked NCAA Division 1 athlete. I was also an accounting major and a two-time track & field national qualifier who essentially got paid to attend college thanks to an abundance of scholarships. Additionally, the day after my speech, I had an all-expenses-paid trip to San Diego, California for an internship interview with one of the top accounting firms in the world! Throughout my speech, I explained how I became this person so they could learn and apply my story to achieve their dreams and versions of success. I also made them critically aware of their environment and possible pitfalls.

I saw how real life could get after high school graduation, and I did not want my audience of students to fall into the same sad cycle that some of my peers had fallen into. While still in high school, my guidance counselor told me and my mother that most students from my school tended to graduate and go away to college for about a semester, only to drop out and come back home due to factors such as limited financial assistance, the fear of their new environment, or the daunting challenge they felt academically and mentally unprepared for. I did not want to believe it until even I became the student who contemplated quitting because of the rigor and financial stress. I have witnessed far too many of my former classmates graduate high school and soon afterward go on to:

1. Unexpectedly have children with unsuitable partners and without being prepared to properly take care of them.
2. Get caught up in illegal activity and then serve years on probation or in prison.
3. Choose jobs or career paths that they hate or work in environments where they feel undervalued.
4. Go away to college for one or two semesters, then drop out and come back home. Most of these students then fall into one or more of the first three categories, or potentially get killed.

Trust me when I tell you that I am not making these things up. Seeing this reality is why I am so passionate about always giving back my time, energy, and encouraging words to current high school students. It pains me to see so many of my former classmates, teammates, friends, and other people I know who are now in jail for drug possession, robbery, or murder. They chose high-risk methods just to get quick cash, but now they are paying hefty prices for their actions.

I promise whoever reads this that nothing is worth giving your life away. Anyone can argue that crime is a product of desperation, but everyone has choices to make. We have been programmed to think that going to jail is normal, acceptable, and "cool." IT IS NOT! I know many former inmates who now wish they did not have a record because of how it still negatively affects their lives. Most schools and jobs require a background check. Once someone is charged with a felony or certain misdemeanors, it limits their options for employment, volunteering, or even attending field trips with their children.

In this same speech, I explained to them my daily schedule and how most days were packed with class, track practice, physical therapy, eating, studying, and meeting with classmates for group projects. I then told them that in order to create the futures they desire, ignorance is no longer an excuse because of their access to information! With all of the technology in their pockets or hands, not getting the answers they need is their own fault. There are many athletes in high school seeking to play their sports at the next level and are waiting for a college coach to send them a letter or come knocking at their door. I advise every student-athlete to be courageous and recognize their power to take the necessary steps to be a part of their own rescue! The advice I gave was: STOP WAITING FOR COLLEGE COACHES TO CONTACT YOU FIRST!

At my high school state track meet during my senior year, I won medals in two events: long jump and high jump. These top eight finishes marked the end of my high school athletic career, but I was still on the journey to becoming a college athlete. The meet was on a Saturday, and on the following Monday, I called and emailed multiple college coaches. I did not wait, cross my fingers, and hope they found me; I went to find them first! How did I reach out to these coaches? Google on my phone and laptop! I logically searched for the college's website, found its athletics page, found the coaches' information, and then used it to contact them. SIMPLE!

This list of colleges includes the University of Cincinnati, Xavier University, Miami University, the University of Akron, and Kent State University. My advice now would be to reach out to more colleges than I did and to broaden your horizon to include different states and divisions. I had just won two medals at the State Championships, won Conference Athlete of the Year, and graduated in the top ten of my class with a 3.7 GPA. That is music to the ears of any college coach, and I leveraged these achievements so they would take me seriously!

I called multiple coaches. None of them answered the phone, but I did not let that stop me. I left each of them a voicemail with my introduction and contact information. After listening to my voicemail, Chad Reynolds, the track coach at Miami University was the first coach to reply. He immediately called me back to schedule a potential campus visit. I also sent emails. This is the actual email message I sent to each coach individually:

Hi Coach. I am Kenny Glenn from Cincinnati Mount Healthy High School, and I compete in the events of high jump and long jump. I am contacting you to find out if there are any spots left or scholarships available on the track team. I made it to State in both events and made it to the podium in both. Please contact me back via this email or call me at 513-XXX-XXXX. Thank you.

I now understand how to send better emails, but this was pretty good for a 16-year-old kid at the time.

I told my audience, and I am telling whoever reads this that you can find the answers to almost any question by simply using resources like Google and YouTube. Just be sure to avoid unreliable or inauthentic sources and learn to identify verified accounts. Most students and graduates waste an unnecessary amount of time scrolling on social media to see what their friends and celebrities are doing, listen to new gossip, or look at nonsense. Now that you are aware, always remember that this behavior is unproductive and will not get you closer to living the life you want. Use your phone and social media to your advantage, to achieve your goals! Social media has made it possible to access and question almost anyone. This reality means that high school athletes can use it to direct message college coaches and athletes. I am using many athletic examples, but you can find ways to apply this to your life if you do not participate in sports. If you seek mentorship or guidance from anyone, use this same mindset shift.

> Dear Kenny,
>
> Be courageous and do what is necessary to achieve your goals. Conducting 15 minutes of research to gather contact information and then send messages to coaches could bring you $150,000 in scholarships. How hard is it for any student-athlete to make a list of 10 to 15 schools and find the coaches' email addresses, phone numbers, and social media pages? How hard is it to introduce themselves and present their GPA, statistics, highlight film, and questions via phone call, email, or direct message? You might think, "What if they don't reply?" In that case, you are no worse off than you were before you sent them a message. But if they do reply, that could change your life and those around you for the better! "All it takes is one!" You only need one reply and one person to provide the necessary opportunity and resources.
>
> Sincerely,
>
> Kenny Glenn, Success Coach and Entrepreneur

Who was in the audience when I gave this speech at my alma mater high school in 2016? The following students who would become overachievers were in attendance:

- **Nahja Glenn** – Salutatorian and two-time graduate of The Ohio State University
- **Trayvon Wilburn** – NCAA Division I Football team walk-on and graduate of The Ohio State University
- **TJ Elliott** – NCAA Division II Track & Field National Champion (while attending Ashland University) and University of Cincinnati graduate
- **CJ Rhodes** – NCAA Division I basketball walk-on at Ohio University, University of Cincinnati graduate, and current professional basketball player

- **Bryan Cook** – NCAA Division I Football All American, University of Cincinnati graduate, and second-round NFL Draft pick for the Kansas City Chiefs
- **Rob Corbin** – NCAA Division II football player and graduate of Central State University

Five and six years after I gave that speech, all of the students listed above had become college graduates! Even if they did not stay at their first schools of choice, and even if some had to return home for a while, they finished what they started. These students have assured me that I am a member of their Mental Hall of Fame. Without me realizing it, this speech was the start of me continually speaking to and inspiring current high school students in public and private settings. It was the crux of this book!

On the same day as this speech, as I was exiting the building, I took a picture of the Mt. Healthy Athletic Hall of Fame on Snapchat and captioned it with "I'm on my way." That was me speaking my dream into existence and then manifesting it through my actions! I had always dreamed of being an unforgettable legend in the eyes of my peers, teachers, coaches, and administrators. A way of achieving this would be my induction into the Mt. Healthy Athletic Hall of Fame. I accomplished this goal when I was officially inducted on January 17, 2020.

CHAPTER 7

Be a Bridge

Work Harder?

Even with all my achievements, degrees, knowledge, and wealth, what good is any of it if I do not give back by inspiring others? I make it a point to give back by speaking to students and graduates while keeping it real! What do I mean by keeping it real? I do not sugarcoat my experiences or the realities of the real world. When wealthy or highly accomplished people are asked how they achieved their status, too often, they only give the default answer of "hard work." Then, they are asked what they did when they failed. The common answer is "try harder." We all know that it is important to work hard, but that is not enough! Thankfully, when my father noticed that I was overworking, he would tell me to "work smarter, not harder." This means you can work hard and make little to no progress while wasting precious time and energy, or you can work smart, be creative, and find efficient ways to arrive at your goal or destination sooner than most.

To elaborate on the point that you need to do more than just "work hard," allow me to use a story told by author, public speaker, and business advisor Price Pritchett about a fly seeking freedom:

A fly was hitting against the glass of a closed window, trying to get out of the room, into the beautiful world outside. It could see lots of other flies outside enjoying complete freedom. The fly was so desperate to become free, that it tried harder and harder to break through the glass.

The whining wings were telling the sad story of the fly's strategy - 'try harder.'

But trying harder was not working.

The fly believed that going through the window was the only way to get to the land of dreams.

The fly eventually died as it kept trying harder and harder to achieve the impossible feat of breaking through glass. Ironically, only a few feet away from the fly, there was an open door that it could have used to free itself. Please use this story to realize that you must expand your mind to create your reality and achieve your definitions of success and freedom. Ask yourself, "Is there a better way to achieve the result I seek?" Try different approaches and find those who are doing or have done what you seek to do, especially the ones who will keep it real and give the full picture.

Alumni Mentorship

The speech I talked about in the previous chapter was my first public effort to reach students, but certainly not my last. I received an amazing feeling by opening the minds and eyes of the students who were following in my footsteps. I also noticed that this was a much-needed solution, as high school students do not see or hear from enough positive alumni figures. I focus on alumni specifically because they usually look like the current students, have similar backgrounds, and previously roamed the same hall-ways. Then, they graduated and went on to be amazing and accomplish what current students dream of.

I personally know dozens of notable alumni from my high school who are succeeding within each of the 4 Es I mentioned in Chapter 3. Many of which I did not attend high school with. They are doing what they love, whether that is working their dream job, owning a profitable business, playing sports at the highest level, or just living a simple but peaceful life. I was "hype" when I learned about these individuals who graduated before me. However, the inquisitive side of me always wondered: "WHERE WERE YOU WHEN I WAS IN HIGH SCHOOL? WHY DIDN'T YOU COME BACK TO SHED LIGHT AND WISDOM ON HOW YOU ACHIEVED YOUR CURRENT STATUS!?" My classmates and I could have greatly benefited from seeing and listening to our alumni periodically.

To be honest, there was one alumnus who came back to speak to us about his success. Diyral Briggs came and gave a speech immediately after he became a Super Bowl Champion with the Green Bay Packers in 2011. Sadly, I do not remember one word he said. I was too busy trying to be "cool" in the back of the auditorium. However, I cannot lightly skip over the fact that he was a professional athlete and part of that 0.0001% of the population. Students and graduates also need to see and hear from alumni who have careers outside of athletics and entertainment. Where are these alumni?

You may wonder where and how I found those who graduated well before me. "The best place to hide anything is to put it in plain sight." Some of these individuals are displayed within the physical school building, by way of the record books, Alumni of the Year photos, and the Athletic Hall of Fame plaques. Those are great ways of displaying what was accomplished by alumni, but I saw the opportunity to take things a step further and search for them on platforms like Facebook and LinkedIn. There were also times when I got lucky and ran into alumni while attending sporting events or shopping around the community. Then, they introduced me to their former classmates or older alumni whom they remembered and were still connected to. The problem, which is no fault of most 13- to 18-year-old students, is they will not make the effort to reach out to these individuals because they may not know what to say or realize that these individuals even exist. This shows the importance of a high school having an updated Alumni Directory that students and graduates can take advantage of. This is a platform that I and my high school class-mate, Russell Rice III, have created for our alma mater.

My personal list of alumni contacts is skewed with athletes because I am an athlete and due to non-athletes sadly going unnoticed. This is a problem in our society as we glorify athletes but overlook people in other professions such as accountants. But the reality is that accountants have longer careers, have easier accessibility, and are needed and used by everyone! Yet, since being an accountant is not popularized as the sexy thing to do, it is rarely celebrated or chosen as a career option. I could easily use other professions and trades as examples for this point.

I challenge the student who reads this to find one or multiple graduates who came from their school and get to know them. Do not limit yourself to five or ten years ago, as there are some alumni who graduated in the 1970s but can still provide you with great wisdom!

I also challenge the graduate who reads this to visit your middle school, high school, college, or local organization and let the students know that you exist and are willing to help or mentor at least one of them. Your profession of choice is not overly important, but your story is! Be honest about the mistakes you have made and the multiple factors that attributed to your success. It is essential for everyone to have mentors for different aspects of life. Mentors help expedite the path toward success.

In some instances, it is okay to lean on one person for multiple topics, but no one is an expert in everything. You are the sum of your network, which includes family, friends, neighbors, employers, classmates, teachers, people you follow on social media, and more. I have a vast network that allows me to make one to two phone calls and get any problem solved or connect with an expert in any field. This network includes, but is not limited to, HVAC experts, plumbers, videographers, investors, life insurance agents, real estate agents, content creators, podcasters, lawyers, medical school students, coaches, professional athletes, teachers at all levels, business owners of all industries and company sizes, and health experts in the physical, mental, and spiritual realms.

Here is an example of a former classmate who achieved his definition of success. Stephon Waters and I grew up together on the same street. Stephon was a class clown who did not play on sports teams or have the best grades. Yet, he had a clear vision for his life after high school, and he brought it to reality. While we were in high school, the night before basketball games, I was able to walk to his parents' house and get a fresh haircut for $5. He cut hair in his basement for many people in our neighborhood and at our school. His basement is also where he built and owned a fully functional music studio. If I wanted to rap or sing after my haircut, I could! Now, more than 10 years later, he is one of the best licensed barbers and music engineers in the Midwest! He also rents a commercial property where he operates both of his passions. Throughout his journey and rise in popularity, he has gained tons of valuable information and knowledge that he now passes on to the next generation. Now, alumni who graduated before, with, and after him are dependent on his expertise. Some may look at him as an overnight success without realizing how long he has been working on his vision and craft. There were even teachers who did not think he would amount to much.

Community Service Events

I hope that readers use the examples and events I give throughout this chapter as hints for what they can do for their communities. If you are passionate about something, create a community event or connect with an existing organization or group of people who share your same passions.

During my last college spring break, I decided to give back to my high school again. Thanks to Mr. Matt White, a college and career readiness teacher, I spoke to his different classes of ninth-grade students for an entire school day. I gave interactive presentations and used an acronym that I created called **FACKTS**. Here is the explanation for each letter:

F = Focus: Intently lock in on whatever mission, goal, or task you have in front of you and do not fall victim to distractions. Focus on your actions and what you need to do to achieve your dreams.

A = Accountability: No more looking for someone else to blame when you fail or fall short! *"GOATs do not go looking for scapegoats!"* When you make a mistake, fail at something, or get rejected, ask yourself, "How can I learn from this and get better?"

C = Confidence: Knowing yourself and believing in your abilities are the biggest factors needed to achieve positive results. If you owned a business, would you rather hire people who doubt themselves or people who believe they can achieve whatever they set their mind to?

K= Knowledge: Your confidence will be backed and strengthened by the knowledge you acquire. Knowledge is gained through experience. Many times in life, you will fail, but most importantly, you will learn! Experience helps you apply what you should do and figure out what you should not do.

T = Time: The present or the NOW (No Opportunity Wasted) will always be the most important time of your life. What you do in the present time determines if you are robbing or investing in your future self. If a student goofs off too much and does not prepare for exams, then fails, it is because they robbed themselves. If that same student chooses to focus and study, then passes any test, it is because they properly invested in themselves.

S = Success: You must create your own definition of what success is and strive towards it with every decision you make! I must capitalize & emphasize this point... **SUCCESS IS SELF-DEFINED!** Society often defines success as your salary and your job title, but trust me when I say it is so much more than that! Success also includes your mental health (peace of mind), physical health, loving what you do, having your loved ones around you, and being able to comfortably enjoy your free time.

Each One, Teach One

Each One, Teach One was an event inspired by Dr. Eric Thomas. One day, he posted a YouTube video of himself and his team inspiring students. They decided to create poster board signs that displayed inspirational messages. I copied this idea and received help from friends and fellow alumni to execute it. I chose the first day of school at each building within my alma mater's school district. As students arrived, they were greeted with positive energy, high fives, smiles, and posters with motivational messages, such as:

"BELIEVE IN YOURSELF AT ALL TIMES!"
"GOOD GRADES ARE WORTH THOUSANDS OF DOLLARS!"
"GREATNESS IS WITHIN YOU!"

91

This event showed the students that we, as a community, supported them and recognized their potential.

On various occasions throughout the school year, I assemble groups of alumni to come speak to current high school students about their journeys. Sometimes the alumni group is all men, all women, or a mixture. College students, business owners, employees, and military personnel are included. These speaking engagements positively impact everyone, as there were instances when speakers were brought to tears upon seeing their former teachers and realizing how far they had come.

Dear Kenny,

Whether you go to college or not, make sure you give back to your community. Help those around you to become better and learn from those who came before you. Be that connecting bridge between the two groups. Also, know that everyone can benefit from giving and receiving helpful advice.

Sincerely,

Kenny Glenn, Success Coach and Entrepreneur

Financial Freedom Fridays

One day, a friend and Miami classmate, Kyle Broadnax emailed me an article, and he suggested that we should teach financial literacy to our community. He explained his reasons, and I agreed with him. There are so many bad habits already instilled in students and graduates due to programming and the lack of proper financial education. Kyle had sent the same email to our classmates Ben Phillips and Rod Mills, as well as our business mentor Dr. J.C. Baker. We ideated and talked about how there were many lessons we had to learn the hard way or rely on books and courses created by people who did not look like us. With Dr.

Baker being certified in finance, he offered to teach financial seminars to our target audience if we could get people to sign up and attend.

This is how we created the event, *Financial Freedom Fridays*. We charged $10 for students and $15 for the public. Some may ask why we charged money to teach about money. The reason was simple: "When people don't pay, they don't pay attention." We were able to pack out rooms, and attendees were happy with the mindset-shifting information they received.

As a transition to the next chapter, I want to again stress the importance of hearing from speakers and having mentors from multiple career paths who have achieved what you seek. Complete the following task:

1. Name five millionaires or billionaires who look like you.
2. Now, do it again. This time, the five you choose are not allowed to be professional athletes or entertainers.

That second list was probably more difficult to complete. But why? It is because we have been programmed to place our values and attention on flashy careers. Even most adults cannot name five millionaires who are not athletes or entertainers. However, please trust me when I say that you do not have to be a criminal, a professional athlete, or an entertainer to become rich or wealthy! There are many other avenues to acquiring wealth and loving what you choose to do. You have the power and creativity to be anything you put your mind to. Money is not the key to happiness, but it sure does help alleviate the stress that not having money brings. There are plenty of five- and six-figure earners who live the lives of their dreams, and students need to hear from them.

Dear Kenny,

Who do you think earns more money per year, Steph Curry or Mark Cuban? If you do not know who these individuals are, Steph Curry is a Hall of Fame basketball player and the best three-point shooter in NBA history. Mark Cuban is a billionaire and the owner of the Dallas Mavericks, an NBA team.

Before becoming a billionaire, Mark Cuban got his first job as a computer software salesman. That job allowed him to learn about technology and how to sell. Afterwards, he created his own company while also investing in the stock market. There are many lessons to be learned from those who did not acquire their wealth from sports or entertainment.

What is stopping you from finding these individuals, questioning them, and then following a similar path?

Sincerely,

Kenny Glenn, Success Coach and Entrepreneur

CHAPTER 8

Financial Literacy

This chapter is important for all groups of people, as finances personally affect all of us. Since I am not a financial advisor, and there are entire books dedicated to finances, I will only focus on the fundamentals. I advise you to find an actual financial advisor.

What comes to your mind when you hear the term "financial literacy?" It has become a popular phrase and topic, and rightfully so. In the 20th century, psychologists theorized that humans' most basic thoughts and motivations could be categorized as The Four Fs: food, fighting, fleeing, and fornicating. I theorize that there is an additional F in the 21st century of commerce and capitalism. We have been taught how to read, how to write, and how to count, but not how to understand the very thing that flows through our minds 24/7. That additional F is for the word... **FINANCES!**

If you are reading this, it is imperative that you adopt the mindset of long-term economic-based thinking. Most of us already do it in some capacity, but we must become more strategic about it. When we make purchasing decisions, large or small, we think, "How much does it cost?" When we gamble or place bets, we think, "How much money can I win?" When we are offered a job or income-producing opportunity, we think, "How many hours do I need to work so I can make X amount of dollars?" Obtaining and spending money is an example of the Universal Law of Reciprocity. You cannot receive without giving. The subject of economics explains it in simple terms: "There is no such thing as a free lunch." If someone gifted you with your favorite meal for zero dollars, it still would not be free because it will cost you something. That something is your time to eat the meal and your bodily energy to chew and digest the food. If time is money, then the time you spend eating might cost you the money you did not earn.

However, it is never enough just to make money, as there are millionaires who still live check to check. Robert Kiyosaki, author of *Rich Dad, Poor Dad*, explains it perfectly: **"It's not about how much money you make, it's how much money you keep."** I advise you to find programs, seminars, videos, books, and people that will teach you more about financial literacy. Explore topics such as personal investing, company 401K plans, individual retirement accounts (IRA), budgeting, buying cars versus leasing them, and loan repayment in depth. Then, it is your responsibility to apply the information you learn. Two simple reads that helped me learn the basics of financial management are the books *Why Didn't They Teach Me This in School: 99 Personal Money Management Principles to Live By* (Cary Siegel) and *No Debt Zone: Your 9 Step Guide to a Debt Free Life* (Ashley Brewster).

Dear Kenny,

If you want to be a millionaire, you can learn from current millionaires and people with no money at all. From the millionaire, you will learn how they obtained their money by thinking, working, investing, believing, visualizing, and networking. From the person with no money, you will learn what you should avoid doing so you do not reach those same results.

Be conscious that as individuals, even though we all have our own paths, some overlaps and life aspects relate to all of us. I challenge you to find and reach out to people who are doing or have already done what you are trying to do. This includes realms beyond just finances.

Sincerely,

Kenny Glenn, Success Coach and Entrepreneur

Blowing Your Money Away?

As of 2021, multiple sources like CNBC and Forbes state that between 60% and 70% of all Americans are living paycheck to paycheck. Even those making over $100,000 a year fall victim to this same statistic. Well, why is that? It is the same reason people who hit the lottery or play professional sports end up broke so quickly. They are financially illiterate and immature. If you do not have the proper mindset, good habits, and discipline when you have a little bit of money, you are bound to repeat the same cycle when your amount of money increases.

Think about how we have been programmed to think about and treat money. Songs with lyrics like "spend a check and get it right back" do not help us adopt habits of proper money management. In my younger days, my father would say "you must have a hole in your pocket" because once I received money, I would immediately spend it all on trivial items. This is what many people do as soon as they receive their paychecks. It's like we have an itch to spend money once we get paid or the weekend hits. Please take the time to remove yourself from this draining cycle.

You must ask yourself, *"Do I have the habits and thoughts of a poor person or a rich person?"* I hear many people say they do not want to be rich because it comes with too many problems. My counterargument is that no matter what someone decides to be, every choice comes with consequences. Wouldn't it be nice to comfortably afford whatever you want to have or give to others? Does it not feel better to be a lender than a borrower?

Just as there are problems that come with being rich, there are problems that come with being poor. By choosing not to be rich you are inherently choosing to be poor. This then leads you to only blame yourself for complaints such as "The rich just get richer" or "I don't have the money to do what I truly desire." Since everything costs money, not only would it make sense to have more knowledge about it, but also to have an abundance of it.

Friends and family will ask me, "Hey Kenny, you're a finance guy. How do I save money?" My literal response is "Don't spend it." This remark could be taken as funny or rude, but it is true. Scratching beneath the surface, note that people are really asking: "How can I get a clearer picture of my spending habits?" This comes down to the type of lifestyle they want and what purchases they consistently make. Just because you CAN afford something, does not mean that you SHOULD buy it.

Before you buy anything, truly think about it and ask yourself, *"Why am I spending this money?"* Is it for basic living necessities? External validation by keeping up with the Joneses or trying to impress others? Sex? Unhealthy addictions? Short-term happiness? Appeasements for childhood or current trauma? Things that will help you achieve your dreams and definition of success? Joyful and memorable experiences?

Have some patience and restraint and think about your purchases from a long-term perspective. Let us use buying a brand-new car as an example. I know that a brand-new car looks nice, and you will impress your friends and neighbors by having it. But think about everything else that it comes with, including at least five years of monthly car payments if you do not pay for it upfront. Also, think about the other expenses attached to the new car, such as higher insurance. If you already have a car that runs just fine, continue to drive it until you can comfortably afford another one.

Dear Kenny,

This is not just financial advice, but life advice: Do not make decisions or purchases impulsively or impatiently. Just because it is heavily marketed and looks good does not mean that it will be good for you. Not everything you see or think you want is worth your attention or money. Live below your means and know that you do not have to impress anyone.

Sincerely,

Kenny Glenn, Success Coach and Entrepreneur

Sources versus Streams

For most people to achieve financial freedom, retire comfortably, or achieve millionaire status, they will need multiple sources and streams of income. Be sure to know the difference between sources and streams of income, then go find the best ones that work for you to live a life of financial abundance. Ashley Brewster outlines it perfectly in her book, *No Debt Zone: Your 9 Step Guide to a Debt Free Life*. Here is the exact excerpt:

"The average millionaire has three sources of income. Within those sources, they have seven streams of income. Having one source is almost like gambling because if you lose your job, you risk diving into debt. By diversifying your sources of income and adding income producing streams, you have other options to get paid.

The main sources of income are earned, passive, and residual. Earned income requires you to do some work in order to be paid. Passive income requires only capital and then your money will begin to grow on its own so long as it is invested in income producing assets such as stocks, real estate, or equity within a company. Residual income comes from creating a product or idea once and then you receive payments from doing the work one time. This income is often in the form of books, royalties, or a product.

It is good to have all three sources and then create streams within those sources. For example, if you have a full-time job and a side hustle of cutting grass, you have earned income. Both would be the same source but different streams. Having a second source would be writing a book and having it sell over and over again, this would be residual. Whatever you decide to do, understand increasing and diversifying your income is no longer a choice, but a necessity."

The Social Media Effect

Social media affects our minds and then our pockets, as it is where comparisons continue to rise after graduating. We start focusing on where people are traveling, what new car they are buying, what house they are buying, and what business they are starting. The updates on what your peers are doing can be fun, but the non-stop comparison is not! This is true personally and financially. Do not be fooled by what is shown to you on social media.

Personally, some people look at my life and think I spend lots of money because of how much I travel. If someone felt envious and wanted to replicate my life, they would probably spend way more than I do. When I travel, the only things I typically pay for are my flight and food. My expansive network of family, friends, former classmates, and teammates allows this reality. In most situations, they let me stay with them and even let me use their cars to get around.

Financially, let me be the one to tell you that you do not need to have every stream of income under the sun to obtain financial freedom. Building wealth takes time, and the time will increase your gratitude for the abundance. STAY AWAY FROM SCAMS OR GET-RICH-QUICK SCHEMES. Anything that comes too quickly, won't last because it will be gone just as quickly as it came. Some social media "gurus" or those trying to get rich quick might tell you to quit your job and rent your car on Turo, buy and flip houses, do Forex trading, sell apparel, own a home healthcare agency, and own a trucking company, ALL AT THE SAME TIME! Who has time to learn and understand these revenue streams while trying to figure out their life during the early stages of adulthood!? Just because new streams of income seem to be working for one or some of your peers does not mean it will work for you. I am not advising you to avoid learning or taking risks, but I implore you to be patient and do your research instead of blindly jumping into anything.

Sex is Expensive

Sexual energy is the most powerful energy in the universe because it is stimulating, satisfying, and used to create life. However, do not allow yourself to be controlled by it! A person who can control their emotions and their sexual energy is power-ful beyond measure! They are truly on the road to achieving their deepest desires!

From a sexual standpoint, it is unbelievable how much money we spend to have sex. I am not referring to direct payments and prostitution. I am referring to when men buy flashy and overly priced items to attract women to have sex with them. Women also buy and wear certain types of clothes to attract men for sex. Both genders consciously or subconsciously think, "They're going to see what I have on and want to have sex with me." It is funny how we will make certain purchases and body configurations to attract sex, but then get mad when we realize certain people only want us because of our money or body. Yet, when we make decisions based on sex, that's exactly what we are purposefully boasting about and seeking to attract.

Whether it be by mistake, or on purpose, the dollar amount we spend because of sex increases drastically once children are created from having unprotected sex. Newsflash: Raising children is expensive! Make smart decisions when you have sex and be cautious about who you have sex with.

> Dear Kenny,
>
> Unprotected sex may feel good, but the potential consequences of diseases or the financial responsibilities of having a child will not feel good. As a teenager or young adult, you may subconsciously think: "My parents had me when they were young, and I turned out alright. So I can be just like them, and my child will be just fine." My response is: "Did you really turn out alright?" If your parents were more financially secure and more mature, could they have provided you with a better life and more opportunities? What kind of reality do you want for your kids? I think we can all agree that it would be wise to have a financial cushion before bringing children into this world.
>
> Sincerely,
>
> Kenny Glenn, Success Coach and Entrepreneur

Going Out?

In America, especially in college, a huge culture centered on going out to party and celebrate for no legitimate reason exists. These people spend money at bars and clubs every weekend and even during weekdays just to feel free and get out of the house. They think, "It has been a long week. I deserve to have fun and treat myself." Yes, it is good to have fun and enjoy life, but there is no need for mindless spending to celebrate every weekend. Those dollars begin to add up quickly. When someone in or out of college chooses to go out, they typically spend money on something, such as paying for an Uber, parking, bar or club entry, alcoholic drinks sold at a premium, and late-night food.

Living that kind of lifestyle every weekend or multiple times a week is costly and overrated! Thanks to Domino's pizza coupons given at college basketball games, I spent many college weekends buying a whole pizza for $1.25 and watching Netflix. If you are working a job, in school, or working towards your goals, weekends can be your time to mentally and physically recharge while saving your money. I understand the social aspect of going out and the fun people have when they do it, but it is not worth doing every weekend.

Dear Kenny,

Do not go out for the approval of others. If you do go out, you do not have to spend money on drugs or alcohol. It is perfectly okay to be yourself and make your own decisions about what to put inside of your body. If people think you are lame because of it, OH WELL! The same reasons that some people will dislike you are the same reasons that other people will love you.

Many people crave scenes where their peers will be because they are afraid to spend time alone. Please do not be afraid to be with yourself sometimes. Self-care and alone time are absolutely necessary!

Sincerely,

Kenny Glenn, Success Coach and Entrepreneur

Free?

Know that everything comes with a cost; for even freedom is not free. All decisions will cost you money, time, or peace of mind. We are conditioned to be impatient and overindulging consumers instead of producers who adopt economic-based long-term thinking. Here is an example that I have seen countless times from students and graduates:

When students and graduates are preparing for life after school, they realize they have the option to no longer live under their parents' roofs or rules. This brings feelings of excitement because they get to move out and be "free." But how free?

Let's say a student decides to move out and get their own house or apartment, but they are mentally, financially, and skillfully unprepared. This means they do not have what is needed to acquire an income that does more than just suffice. So now they are living paycheck to paycheck, and they become slaves to their job or jobs. This is because they must spend most of their time at work to pay rent and other concurrent bills. How "free" is that?

I understand that some students and graduates are in situations so drastic that their best choice is to leave their parents, or they plan to move to a different city or state than their parents. In those situations, living together is not feasible. However, if you live in a manageable situation with parents or family members who will listen to you, explain to them that staying with them will allow you to save time and money short-term. You can then properly save and invest your money towards living comfortably in the future. This could be your strategy for a year or two, or for as long as your family allows.

As you enter adulthood and seek freedom, it is wise to create a budget by listing all your income and expenses. Name each expense and put the dollar amount next to it. Here are some examples of adult expenses:

- Rent or mortgage
- Renters or homeowners' insurance
- Food (groceries and restaurants)
- Cable & Internet
- Phone
- Power
- Water
- Gas
- Car payment, insurance, and maintenance
- Parking

- Subscriptions (e.g., Netflix)
- Gym membership
- Clothes
- Flights & Vacations
- Savings & Investing
- Health & Life insurance
- Entertainment (recreation, theaters, athletic events, etc.)
- Mental health and self-improvement

Dear Kenny,

Be wise about where and how you spend your time, money, and energy. Also, please remember that terms like "riches" and "costs" are about more than just dollars, digits, and pieces of gold or paper. How much is your peace of mind worth? How much is your health worth? Unless you accumulated money by investing money or somebody gifted you with money that you do not have to pay back, you probably spent time earning your money. Therefore, you should value it by putting it to good use. Most people frivolously or recklessly spend money that is based on temporary feelings and emotions, the desire to impress others for social status and acceptance, or the desire to attract sexual partners. But how close are overly priced clothes going to get you to your goals of financial freedom?

I understand sometimes you will want to treat yourself to celebrate a long week or certain period of time, but do not make this a bad cycle of blowing your money. Find an inexpensive way to treat yourself and save your money. I am also not saying you must put 100% of your paycheck into a savings account or into investing. But it would be wise and highly beneficial to automatically save a comfortable percentage, between 10 and 30 percent, of your paycheck. Label this as your emergency fund and build that savings account up to at least three months of your monthly expenses. If you spend $2,000 per month to live, then you should have at least $6,000 saved in your emergency fund. A strategy to help you save money is to label it as a monthly expense so it becomes mandatory.

Sincerely,

Kenny Glenn, Success Coach and Entrepreneur

Investing

Your first investment should always be in yourself by ways of mental, physical, and spiritual health & growth. Second, you should invest in your and your family's futures by way of finances and opportunities. I spoke about saving your money, but it is a fact that you cannot save your way to financial freedom. Financially wealthy people do not trade time for money. Instead, they invest in a diverse portfolio of business ventures like private small businesses, public companies listed on the stock market, real estate, and more. You must invest so your money grows well past the rate of inflation. The subject of investing can get very deep, which is why some experts charge thousands of dollars to teach different aspects of it, such as IRAs, 401Ks, and day trading. I will keep it as simple as possible by giving my strategy and only focusing on buying and holding stocks in publicly traded companies.

Dear Kenny,

Put a percentage of the money you save towards investing so your money can grow. There are app platforms like Acorns and Robinhood that will automatically invest portions of your money for you. We were programmed as kids to save all our money in a piggy bank. But the Bible says, "Do not give your pearls to swine." A pig is swine, and if we only saved our money, it would lose its value because of inflation. Save what you need to be comfortable in your emergency fund and checking account, then invest the rest.

Sincerely,

Kenny Glenn, Success Coach and Entrepreneur

Stocks

I began investing in stocks thanks to Joaquin Garza, a high school and college classmate of mine. Joaquin is a financial market genius who has earned great returns from the stock market by investing in the right companies at the right time. He introduced me to the Robinhood platform that allows retail investors to buy stocks without fees! I was nervous at first because the platform asked for my social security number. But he told me that all financial institutions do that for security and tax purposes. There was no way around it, and I did not have to worry about someone stealing my identity. Robinhood also allows its users to buy fractional shares. That means that if one stock of a company is $300 but you only have $50 to invest, you can still buy $50 worth of that stock. This was not accessible to the public 10 years ago.

Since platforms like Robinhood offer fractional shares, there is no excuse for anyone with a phone to not invest at some level. An example of an excuse is iPhone owners saying, "I don't have $200 to buy a portion of or a whole share of Apple stock." But I guarantee you, if it cost $200 for them to get their cracked screen fixed, they would find the $200. Even if someone only had $20 per month to invest, they could buy fractional shares of a company like Apple, and eventually, they would own at least one whole share.

I have had many conversations about which stocks are best to buy and here is my advice on it. KEEP IT SIMPLE! Buy stock in companies that you already use daily or eventually want to use. Also, look around you and see what everyone else is using on a daily basis. When you buy stocks, hold them for the long term and keep emotions out of it! The stock market goes through ups and downs, but it always goes back up. Be patient and know that you do not have to look at your stock portfolio every hour.

In 2017, I purchased stocks in the following companies: Apple, Microsoft, Tesla, Facebook, and Chipotle. They are large companies with genius-level CEOs and worldwide consumer bases, and I use them. I am not saying you must choose these exact companies, but my advice is to invest in the best companies. Do not worry about the companies that are here today and gone tomorrow. Those types of companies produce short-term gains and induce FOMO (fear of missing out) because they are all over the news and social media. Stick with the companies that are constantly growing at a steady pace.

Joaquin Garza was not my only information source about the stock market. I learned even more, thanks to Ashley Brewster. She taught me about ETFs which are exchange-traded funds. Simply put, ETFs are like a mixing pot of multiple stocks that allows for a lower risk of losing money due to diversification. Diversification is important because it reduces your losses when there are temporary dips in the stock market or within one specific industry or company. An ETF with the ticker symbol VOO (which stands for Vanguard 500 Index Fund) has percentages of Apple, Microsoft, Amazon, and other top 500 companies. Purchasing shares of that ETF is like owning small pieces of those companies.

Earn Your Leisure Podcast is another information source about the stock market and businesses. The hosts are two men who started a podcast to teach financial literacy on topics like investing, economic-based thinking, and operating businesses in all industries (technology, real estate, trucking, etc.). Their motto is "assets over liabilities," and their platform has expanded across the globe.

Here is a simple explanation of assets and liabilities. An **asset** puts money in your pocket. A **liability** takes money out of your pocket. You would be surprised at how many fully grown adults don't understand these definitions.

Why did I gravitate to *Earn Your Leisure*? Rod Mills, one of my best friends, referred me to it. The hosts look like me, sound like me, and speak about what I am interested in learning. They also did it on their terms while wearing sweatsuits and sneakers. We were taught that "success" and smart people must wear suits all the time, but this is not true.

Dear Kenny,

Investing can be a rabbit hole, but while you are young, just focus on the basics. Do not get swayed by the get-rich-quick schemes that you see. When attempting to learn something like the stock market, make it relatable to you. Put it in terms you understand or ask whoever is teaching you to do so.

Sincerely,

Kenny Glenn, Success Coach and Entrepreneur

Credit and Debt

This topic should be taught in schools and especially at home! The problem occurs when parents or teachers do not understand credit or have good credit. Think about the things we use credit for: to purchase houses and cars, get jobs in certain industries, get approved for apartments, as well as get approved for personal and business loans. We have been scared away from credit, but America runs on it. Some people will tell you to completely stay away from credit cards because they can be seen as a scam. I am not one of those people because I see the benefits and uses of credit.

If you are new to credit, you might think about and say what you have heard from others such as, "I am afraid of maxing out credit cards and getting into debt." The solution is simple. Do not max out your credit card. ONLY SPEND WHAT YOU CAN AFFORD! Then, pay your credit card bill in full each month to AVOID THE MINIMUM PAYMENT so you can avoid paying unnecessary interest! With credit cards, it is also wise to keep your utilization low. For example, if you have a card with a $1,000 limit, do not spend above 30% or $300 on that card per month. A way to build credit other than credit cards is making payments on time, whether they are for car payments, rent, bills, or school and business loans.

Credit building activities are the same reasons some people go into debt. Debt is all about leverage and having a legit plan to pay it back. **There are not many things more stressful than owing someone money. So it is wise to avoid bad debt for foolish situations.** Debt can be good if necessary for situations like school or solid business ideas that will benefit your future. Discipline and timeliness are the top factors when it comes to credit and debt. The most important thing about credit is not your credit score, but your credit report. Keeping a clean credit report should be your priority! You must be responsible to pay bills and loan payments on time. You must also make sure you do not max out any credit cards. Instead, pay the full balance before the due date. Credit card companies are hoping you carry an unpaid balance or forget to pay so they can make money by charging interest. However, most credit cards are connected to banks with phone apps to simplify paying the full balance. You can set up automatic payments so you do not even have to think about it.

While I was in college, my father gave me and my sister our own credit cards for typical everyday expenses. He told me that whatever I formerly bought with my debit card, I could now purchase with my credit card instead. Then, he instructed me to immediately pay my balance in full every month so I would not need to pay any interest. This small change brought big rewards as it would allow me to establish and build a solid credit report that I could leverage for future purchases. Here is another benefit of using credit cards. If you were walking in a dark alley with $10,000, would you rather it be the money that you worked hard for or the bank's money that they let you use? I ask this question because fraud occurs with the use of card information every day. If fraud occurs, the process to retrieve the funds is much easier with a credit card than with a debit card. I rarely use my debit card, and when I do, it is usually to retrieve cash from ATMs. Whenever possible, I use one of my credit cards for my purchases.

Average?

I understand that not everyone wants to be as rich and famous as Elon Musk because of the non-glamorous things that are attached to having that much money and attention. Most people just want to be healthy, be happy, be loved by those close to them, make a decent wage, drive a nice car, and live in a safe neighborhood. We have a current notion that there is something wrong with average, but it depends on the category or the situation. Having an average range is the way the universe works as there is a literal law of averages! There is an average height, average weight, average income, average number of books read by wealthy people, and an average number of hours spent on a task to become an expert. Yes, there will always be outliers that fall into the categories of extremely below or above average, but there must be an average for there to even be a "below" or an "above."

Most people would be upset if someone called them average without any context or legitimate comparison. But would those same people be upset if they were labeled as average billionaires? The description of average becomes problematic when it is taken out of context, the data is misleading, or the comparison is deemed unfair. Numbers do not lie, but they do not tell the whole story. Do not be misled by the term "average."

Dear Kenny,

Know that you we uniquely created, and just like a snowflake, there is no one else out there who is exactly like you. You are not average; it is your actions, descriptions, and possessions that may be labeled as average. In terms of finances, do your best to make sure that you and your family can live comfortably. If you are comfortable with average, then accept that. BUT DO NOT HATE ON THOSE WHO CHOOSE TO POSSESS AND ACHIEVE ABOVE AVERAGE! We all make decisions that lead us to who and what we want to be. What will you choose?

Sincerely,

Kenny Glenn, Success Coach and Entrepreneur

SECTION 4: COLLEGE

To think that in such a place,
I led such a life.

— MIAMI UNIVERSITY
ADOPTED QUOTE

CHAPTER 9

The Transition to College

Earlier, I explained my high school experience and college preparation process in terms of academics and athletics. In this chapter, I offer some simple transitioning tips for those who choose to attend college. This statement may seem like a contradiction, but as a college graduate and athlete, I can honestly say that you do not have to be either to be "successful." Success is a self-defined word anyway! Since I am both, I can also say that college academics and college athletics significantly increased my options of achieving my personal definition of success. Find what will best help you, and do not limit or doubt yourself.

Is College Worth It?

You will have to determine that answer for yourself based on the information that I and others give you. Based on my opinion, perspectives, and experiences, I think college is worth it **IF** leveraged correctly. Although I see the BS that colleges sell and put students and graduates through, I do not regret my choice! It was one of the best decisions I have ever made, and I am truly blessed and grateful for my experience. College expanded my mind, my perspectives, my career options, and my network! Thanks to attending and graduating from Miami University, I have lifelong memories and connections with so many great people on an ever-expanding list. College is about more than the piece of paper they give you after you earn the necessary grades and credit requirements. College is about the experience and the connections you make with your peers, your professors, the alumni who came before you, and those who will come after you. I had no idea about certain companies, internships, or available roles until I arrived at college. Attending Miami University also allowed me to be surrounded by 16,000 other students who were around my same age and all seeking to advance their lives.

If I had not gone to college, I probably would have stayed in Cincinnati and been comfortable with only knowing family members, friends from high school, and eventual coworkers. I could make a phone call and ask, "Hey bro, I'm visiting your area. Is it cool if I spend the night?" My high school friend would say "Yes," and then I would drive for 25 minutes from Uptown Cincinnati to Downtown Cincinnati. But with college, came massive expansion! Now, my personal and professional networks reach across the entire globe. I call friends who live in different states and countries, and then I book flights to visit them.

Whenever I am in Ohio, I purposefully wear Miami University apparel, no matter if I am going to the grocery store, to the gym, or to an event. I do this because someone is bound to see the logo and ask if I went to Miami. That sparks a fun conversation because either they or someone they know went to Miami and talk about how great the experience was. Now that is another person I have connected with and could potentially learn from or help.

Helpful Tips

In this section, I will share some helpful tips for maximizing your college preparation and college career. **Compare your college choices** and see what certain schools offer that others do not. When choosing a college, know that it is a bidding war, and it is your responsibility to list the pros and cons of each. Colleges around the world are selling you on the reason why you should attend their institution versus others. This comparative list includes financial aid and tuition cost, what is the college known for, majors they offer, notable alumni, graduate job placement, updated facilities, safety being a top priority, guest speakers, student organizations, etc. Also, think about the **travel expenses** you or someone will have to pay when you want to go home for holidays and breaks.

Where Do I Start?

Aside from choosing a school in-state versus out-of-state, or public versus private, another financial decision is choosing what type of institution you want to begin your college career at. You could choose to go straight to a four-year university and pay the premium price that comes with it. Or you could choose to attend a community college or branch campus during your first two years and then transfer to a four-year university to complete your major and bachelor's program. The classes are typically the same during the first two years, but the experience is much different. Choosing the community college or branch campus option will save you money, but you will miss the full experience larger universities offer.

Financial Aid

College is expensive. No matter where you choose to attend college, my advice is to apply for every **scholarship** under the sun! Ask local organizations like fraternities and sororities, your parents' jobs, and local churches if they have scholarships you can apply for. Use every resource available to you—including your teachers, guidance counselors, administrators, college students and graduates, and Google—to help you find scholarships. If you are lazy like I was in high school, there are even scholarships you can apply for without needing to write an essay. Surprisingly, there are also scholarships for characteristics like being left-handed, being of a certain ethnicity, or being of a certain height. The list is endless, and millions of dollars go unclaimed every year because not enough students apply for them.

Be sure to ask your counselors, mentors, and teachers to help you properly fill out the **FAFSA** form. FAFSA stands for Free Application for Federal Student Aid, and it helps schools determine what types of financial aid and how much aid students are eligible to receive based on personal and parental demographics and finances. After my sophomore year, I was awarded a $14,000 Pell Grant which came from properly and continuously completing my FAFSA before each school year.

You can apply for scholarships every year of your college tenure, not just before your first year. During my first year, all my scholarships were based on academics and did not fully cover my room and board costs. Before my second year, to help pay for the rest of my college tenure and fully cover all expenses, I earned a partial athletic scholarship thanks to my stellar athletic performance and from speaking to the right people. Going into my fourth year of college, I applied for and received a $1,000 scholarship from Kappa Alpha Psi Fraternity, Incorporated which helped pay for off-campus expenses like groceries and gas.

Employment

Employment while in college can be helpful. A student can get a job on campus or near campus to help pay for college tuition or other living expenses. A great option is becoming a resident assistant after freshman year to receive free housing. Other on-campus options include working in dining halls, becoming a tutor, or a teacher's assistant to receive pay and other useful benefits.

Health

Take your physical health seriously. I have witnessed former classmates gain the infamous "Freshman 15" pounds and then turn that into the "Senior 60" pounds. Many students eat unhealthy foods and binge alcoholic drinks to alleviate stress, which comes from their rigorous course load. Please know that your body is a temple and that "you are what you eat." If you eat like trash, how do you expect your mind and body to feel? On college campuses, there will be a plethora of food options as well as a plethora of exercise options. Actions such as simply walking or biking around campus instead of riding the bus or electric scooters can help to keep you physically active.

Finding Mentors

Just like any other area in life, mentors can help you reach your definition of success much sooner! For college success, this includes knowing which classes and professors to avoid, what types of organizations you should join, and who can help you find employment. Your college mentors could be current college students, recent college graduates, professors, or staff members.

These groups of people have already gone through what you are seeking to do. Just like the premise of this book, they have helpful advice to give you. Avoid bumping your head.

Community

Build a community. College campuses have all types of fun and informative groups and organizations for you to join that align with your passions and interests. These groups will allow you to build your community of friends who come from various backgrounds. Here are examples of different organizations: chess club, campus recruiting, community service, investing, student government, intramural sports, Greek-lettered organizations, campus ministry, singing groups, and more! If your college does not offer a group that you would want to join, create your own!

Textbooks

Buy your course textbooks only if you absolutely need them for certain classes after two weeks into the semester. This tip can save you thousands of dollars! Even if you earned a scholarship to pay for textbooks, use those funds for something else. Your first step when starting class is to go through your syllabus and figure out how much you will even need to read the textbook. Then, find and become friends with classmates who already have the textbook, especially if that classmate is on a full-ride scholarship with textbooks included. I had a class that wanted me to pay $300 to read only 20 out of 300 pages the whole semester!!! Instead of wasting my money, I found a student on a full-ride scholarship and asked them if I could take pictures of the pages I needed in their book. They kindly allowed me to, as they also would not have paid the unnecessary expense if they had to.

If that strategy does not work, there are a few ways that you can still save some money on textbooks. Campus & local libraries might have the books you need. You must try to check them out as soon as you register for your classes because libraries will only have a limited quantity, if any at all, and some of your peers will have the same idea. Renting is also cheaper than buying if that option is available. You can shop around online instead of assuming that you can only buy or rent textbooks from the campus bookstore. This approach works unless the campus bookstore has exclusive rights to certain books, including custom-made books and specific editions. If you order online, you cannot procrastinate if you want to make sure you receive your books before you need them.

Major Decision

I vaguely mentioned **choosing a major** earlier in the book, but it is imperative that I discuss it here as well. Please put some serious thought into choosing your major. Most college students change their majors at least once, just as I did. Also, just because you graduate in a certain major does not mean you must work in, or can only work in, that field or industry. A large percentage of college graduates choose different career paths than what they earned their degrees in. You might choose a major that you are passionate about, but you or the general masses do not currently see the financial benefit. This is an example of how college is about leverage and networking! As early as possible, find others who have graduated with your major of choice and ask them how they leveraged their degrees. Lastly, it would be wise to choose a major that aligns with an industry that will eventually or always be needed, such as education, mental and physical healthcare, technology, law, business, and engineering.

Your Time and Self-Discipline

Create a schedule and implement daily habits to instill self-discipline. You are in charge of your time. You get to choose if you want morning, afternoon, or night classes. A planner, print or electronic, is one of the most valuable tools you can have in college. Create a schedule for your days so you do get blindly pulled in every direction. However, maintain some flexibility and allow for some spur-of-the-moment occurrences. It is also important to schedule breaks, naps, and times to have fun! Good daily habits that instill discipline can be as simple as making your bed, writing in a gratitude journal, planning your meals, and creating a to-do list.

Find time for yourself. During your first year on campus, you will probably have a roommate. Try your best to get along with this person but still find time to be alone. Being alone has great benefits such as time to be more productive, adapt to your new environment, and explore personal interests. During your alone time, it would be best to find "balance." Balance is a personal tightrope because there are times when you will lean heavily into certain aspects while neglecting others, and vice versa. What seems like balance for you, might seem off balance for someone else and that is OKAY! Some students want to study on Sundays but party every Saturday to release their stress, some students want to study every day while also exercising for two hours a day. Do what is best for you.

Find a hobby. College is not about studying 24/7, as that would quickly lead to burnout. Your hobby can be anything that you think is fun and that can free your mind when you are not in class, studying, or at an event. Your hobby can be something you choose to keep private or share with the public. If you choose to share it publicly, understand that negative criticism may follow, but do not allow it to stop you. Outsiders may be jealous of your courageous acts and assume you are trying to become famous with your hobby. Take making music, for example. Maybe, you are just having fun with what you produce. People who feel the need to voice their opinions may say things like "They shouldn't be doing that" or "They are no good and should just stop trying." Avoid becoming this type of person or letting these types of people dim your light. They subliminally think of themselves as unworthy. So they attempt to cast that same energy onto others. Let people live their lives and do not be afraid to live yours!

Coursework

Use voice recording while you take handwritten notes. You are much more likely to remember something when you write it down. The importance of note-taking extends way beyond the classroom, as you may attend an event or have an impactful conversation that you do not want to forget. However, there is no way you can capture everything while you are listening to your professor or presenter. In the age range of 15 to 50, I estimate a large percentage of individuals have a phone that allows them to use a voice recording app. While attending an informational event, visiting a campus, or sitting in a class, you can record and save what is being said. Voice recording not only allows you to go back and listen to what you could not write down, but also to dissect what was said whenever you please. This option allows you to receive all the information that you may not have remembered or had time to write down. Just be careful to avoid accidentally pressing "play" instead of "record" when you are in class.

Take advantage of office hours with your professors and teacher's assistants. Never be ashamed to get any extra help you need from your professors during office hours. There are some classes, like business statistics, that I would not have passed without going to office hours. Avoid procrastination. A common example is waiting until you are completely lost in a class before reaching out for help. Another example is showing up at the professor's office when office hours are almost over. Professors have schedules, too. They need to leave their office hours on time so they can be on time for their classes, meetings, or other obligations. If it seems necessary or more helpful than dropping in, make an appointment to meet with your professor.

Speak with your advisors frequently to make sure you are on the proper track to graduate. Your advisors are also beneficial to talk to before you make impactful decisions like changing your major or dropping a class. I originally thought having a "W" on my transcript would be frowned upon by future employers. However, it just means that a student has withdrawn from a course, and many students do this for various reasons. If you are convinced that you will earn a final grade lower than a "C," withdrawing is probably your best option. Do not wait until the last minute to decide. Consider the difficulty level of your other classes and whether you can withdraw from one class without losing your full-time student status. It is also important to find out when the course will be offered again if it is a graduation requirement. The designation you want to avoid when dropping a class is "WF," which means that you have missed the "W" deadline and that you are only withdrawing to avoid receiving an "F."

Find credit transfer opportunities! My advisors also helped me to find classes I could take online during the summer through different colleges. By doing this, the passing grade I earned would not matter! All I needed to do was pass the summer course to receive the same credits towards graduating. I transferred my economics courses and a business law course. If a student knows they struggle in a certain class or subject, it would be wise to use this transfer option. Find out which courses you are allowed to transfer and do not exceed the number of credits you are allowed to transfer.

When studying for exams, find peers who understand the material and ask them to help you or even form a study group. A tip that helped me tremendously was studying in the area where you will eventually take the test. Many times, I studied in the actual classroom where I would take my exams. I even sat in my actual seat so I could be fully prepared.

Finals week! College is heavily focused on exams, group projects, papers, and presentations, especially near the end of each semester. These are some reasons why finals week is a highly stressful time for most students. I advise you to prepare for final exams well before the end of each semester.

Keep your self-talk positive! You should be your biggest fan and you should speak to yourself in a positive manner. There will be times when you feel depressed or lack motivation. These are the times when it is most beneficial to give yourself a pep talk with "I Am" affirmations. Here are some examples:

"I am smart." "I am amazing." "I am enough."
"I am capable of successfully completing any assignment."
"I am resourceful, and I can find the solution to any problem."
"I am on the path to graduating from college."

125

Read for pleasure and self-development. Find books that align with your interests or areas you want to improve. It is highly crucial to your success that you read more than just what your professors assign to you. Reading allows your mind to wander and slow down. This is crucial as we are in the digital age of fast-paced living and constant downloads of information and propaganda.

It is up to you to decide which of these tips you will adopt. In closing, I offer some additional high-level points for you to consider. In 2012, Jullien Gordon gave a TEDx speech entitled "How to graduate college with a job you love & less debt." I suggest that all readers find and watch this video on YouTube. Whether you watch it or not, I will summarize the four points he emphasized at the end of the speech when determining if college is worth it. With any major, self-discipline leads to self-mastery. Take calculated risks outside of the classroom as you will learn from your successes and your failures. Learning life lessons is just as important as meeting the criteria required for your graduation. Last but not least, college is an investment into your dream, and an opportunity to expand your network; it is not a job guarantee.

CHAPTER 10

My Freshman and Sophomore Years

Adjustment Phase

I enjoyed being a wide-eyed freshman as things were happening so quickly, and it was all new to me. This was my first time living away from home and being around so many people who did not look like me. My roommate was the literal opposite of me in more ways than just appearance. It seemed like all he wanted to do was party and drink every night with his future frat brothers. I quickly realized there was only one other Black male student in my entire dorm, but he eventually moved out. Thankfully, my resident director was a cool Black man, named Julian Oliver. He became a mentor and a big brother figure by being someone to talk with and receive guidance from. He and I are still close friends today!

The first week and weekends on any college campus are party time every single day and night! This week is called syllabus week because this is when professors review their course syllabi and typically do not give any assignments yet. I initially met my teammates during syllabus week at the track and at the unofficial "track house" where some of my teammates lived and threw parties. Before one of those parties, a teammate asked me if I drank alcohol. I was 17 years young and completely lied to him by saying "yes" because I wanted to try it for the first time. He handed me a beer and it was the most disgusting thing I had ever tasted.

Fortunately, I had a teammate, Adam Bodrick, who would become another mentor and big brother figure. Adam let me know it was okay to casually drink alcohol that tastes good or even choose to not drink. He also showed me how I did not need to attend every party or accept every invitation to go out and get drunk. This was a major relief as the number one question I would hear every day from at least one person on campus was "Are you going out tonight?" They asked in an inviting way, but I was always amused by the consistency. Most times, I would say "no" and give them a strange look because it was usually a school night. I was conscious of having class at 8:30 a.m., exams to study for, a high GPA to accomplish, and a need for proper rest for track practice. Why would I repeatedly go out and jeopardize all of that? There were some nights when I said "yes" to partying during the week and weekends. However, I learned that frequent partying soon becomes repetitive and less interesting, as it typically involves the same chain of events and people in attendance. "Going through the motions" just to fit in simply is not worth it. Have fun when it is practical and if you can be responsible, but always prioritize your studies and your future.

Dear Kenny,

There will always be outside pressures pulling at you to be like everyone else and just fit in with the norm. But who decides what normal or cool is? At the end of the day, you always must look yourself and your morals in the mirror. Your positive and higher self (mind, body, and spirit) will help you decipher between right and wrong. Here's an example: "Kenny, most of your classmates and teammates are excessively partying, smoking, drinking, and eating unhealthy food. You should do it, too." My response: "SKIP THAT! How do those things help me live a better life or achieve my goals? I refuse to blindly follow the masses and I choose to think for myself while carving my own path of greatness!"

Sincerely,

Kenny Glenn, Success Coach and Entrepreneur

As an athlete with a high metabolism, I was always hungry! Yet, thanks to my father trying to save every penny of the $10,000 he paid for me to stay in a dorm on campus, I was forced to choose the cheapest meal plan available. This led me to rely on other athletes to swipe me into dining halls so I could save my little bit of money for food when I was alone. Freshman and sophomore athletes on the football team and basketball team quickly became my homies! I also had a cousin on the football team, Kelvin Cook, who always looked out for me. Since he and most of the other athletes lived in the dorm across from mine, I spent lots of time over there. We ate together, partied together, and played video games. Also, since I was the only Black track male athlete who lived on campus, they provided the social connection I needed. Some of those guys have become beneficial lifelong friends, such as the former professional basketball player, Rod Mills.

Often, I had to rush to class after practice or rush to practice after class. Walking was entirely too slow to get around on the large campus of Miami. This led to me riding my bike all over campus. Having a lock was extremely necessary because a bike without a lock would be stolen. I bought multiple cheap locks because I did not have or want to spend much money. As the days got colder, my lock eventually froze, and I was done buying new ones just for the same thing to happen again. My creative solution was to get to class early, enter a side entrance of the building, and carry my bike down the stairwell to the basement. When I first implemented this idea, I wrote on a piece of paper: "Entrepreneur Project! DO NOT TOUCH OR REMOVE!" I also wrote the name of the professor who headed the entrepreneurship program. This helped make sure no student or staff member would touch my bike. Genius right!?

Freshman Year: Academics

I wanted to treat college just like high school and establish a good GPA to build a solid foundation. In most classes, I immediately noticed I was the only Black student and the only athlete. Therefore, it was easy for everyone to remember my name, but there were many times when I felt like I did not belong. I thought to myself, "The other students probably think I'm just a dumb jock who is fulfilling the minority quota." This is called imposter syndrome. First and foremost, I had to remind myself that I was in college thanks to my academic prowess, with the hopes of eventually earning an athletic scholarship. Still, even with all the advanced classes I passed in high school and the college summer programs I attended during my youth, I still felt unprepared.

Certainly, I would have felt more comfortable at a Historically Black College or University (HBCU), but I was at Miami University, a Predominately White Institution (PWI). The percentage of students at Miami University who identified as Black Americans was only 3%! However, thanks to my high school having a 90% Black American student population, that was my version of an HBCU experience. Attending a PWI for college forced me to develop the ability to adapt and succeed in any environment. This reality exposed me to different cultures and backgrounds as well as new levels of wealth. While on campus, I casually saw luxurious cars made by Lamborghini, Bentley, Porsche, and

Maserati, to name a few. Before then, I was only accustomed to seeing cars made by Honda, Toyota, and Nissan.

Dear Kenny,

The college adjustment period is a situation where it is applicable to "fake it till you make it" to overcome imposter syndrome. I began to act like I belonged until I felt and realized I truly did. I deserved to be in those same classrooms, and I had the same right and ability to complete assignments. Now, when I walk into any room or building, I act as if I belong there. This aura can be felt by everyone around me, and it prevents questions like, "Sir, can I help you" or "Are you lost?" If I walked around timidly and showed it on my face, I would stick out for the wrong reasons.

Sincerely,

Kenny Glenn, Success Coach and Entrepreneur

Another factor that attributed to me being uncomfortable during my adjustment phase was the fact that I did not study for any exams in high school. This quickly changed in college after I failed my first exams in physics and calculus. I withdrew from physics because I no longer wanted to continue the path of being a mechanical engineering major. In calculus, I was nonchalant before the first exam because I took calculus during my senior year of high school. In the beginning, most of the material was the same. So I chose not to pay attention in class. There were some days I even went to sleep if the lesson sounded familiar. I decided to stay in calculus because my advisor told me I would need it for whatever major I eventually chose. In order to increase my grade, I had to intensify my focus and go to office hours at every chance. Most college courses are three credit hours, but calculus was five! This meant the grade I earned in calculus would weigh more heavily on my GPA than any of my other grades. Thanks to my efforts, I received As and Bs on future calculus exams and earned a B+ as my final grade.

I also did the typical college student thing of pulling an all-nighter on a paper I had to write for English class. This is where I advise avoiding procrastination. It is much easier and less stressful to complete assignments sooner rather than later. I stayed up until 5:00 a.m. typing my paper and then had to attend my 8:30 a.m. class. I could have easily skipped class because my professors were not strict on attendance like high school teachers. However, I did not want to make skipping class a habit or miss out on information that might be on a future exam. I did not feel the effects of my lack of sleep until the next day, and it showed. My coach was able to see my unusual sluggish behavior. This instance was the first and last time I would wait until the last minute to complete an assignment.

Deeper into the semester, I began spending more time with Adam Bodrick and learning more about him during and after practice. When I arrived at Miami, he was a junior and 400-meter specialist. We would eventually link up on Friday and Saturday nights to play basketball in our main arena while everyone else was out partying at the bars. Adam taught me how to balance being a high-GPA student, a finance major, and a great track athlete. He introduced me to Michelle Thomas, the Director for Diversity and Inclusion in Miami University's Farmer School of Business. Mrs. Thomas has been extremely instrumental in helping me and other students get into the business school, choose our majors, and find internships. After switching from being a mechanical engineering major, I contemplated majoring in sports leadership and management like most athletes. Adam and Mrs. Thomas assured me that I was much too smart to choose that major as a cop out to avoid difficult classes.

Then, I chose to major in finance like Adam because I loved numbers and business. One day, a Miami alum told me that majoring in accounting would allow me to learn both finance and accounting. Their advice made sense as I wanted to maximize my major and future job opportunities. Plus, the basics seemed easy to me because I had taken an accounting course in high school. At that point, I decided to become an accounting major.

Dear Kenny,

You are not confined to your major! This not only includes the ability to change it, but also to eventually work outside of your major or degree. I am a prime example of this because I have two degrees in accounting, but it does not mean I must be an accountant. Choosing the business major of accounting at a rigorous school like Miami forced me to learn and grow outside of my comfort zone. I eventually realized that my passion is not tied to accounting, nor do I like the subject! However, I know the importance of it, and now I can leverage my degrees and knowledge of the subject in applicable settings. I must also say that you should not emotionally give up when classes get hard or you fail an exam. Ask yourself if you are truly passionate about what you are studying. I have no regrets about my choice because of the benefits it has provided me and others close to me. However, do not stay in a major just because your parents or peers like and approve of it.

Sincerely,

Kenny Glenn, Success Coach and Entrepreneur

Michelle Thomas is also the liaison for the business group, the Multicultural Business Association (MBA). Adam was an executive member, and he invited me to their weekly meetings where free pizza was always served. Thanks to MBA I gained other mentors such as Glenn Trepeta, Buku Ibraheem, Celena Fields, and Mwoyo Chinoda.

Glenn Trepeta taught me the best questions to ask during an interview. I will list them in the next chapter.

133

Buku Ibraheem kept my spirits high with her energy and inspirational quotes, such as:

> "Failure is just success pending."
>
> "What is meant for you, will happen for you."
>
> "Turn your passion into a paycheck."

With her internship with the NBA Summer League in Las Vegas, Celena Fields helped me see how big the world was and what types of internship opportunities were available.

Mwoyo rewrote and rearranged my entire job résumé to make it top tier. This allowed me to start interviewing with companies I did not even know about beforehand.

Résumé Tips

A résumé is a snapshot of your professional self that you use to get an interview. Typically, it is all typed on one sheet. A bonus tip is to extend the page margins so you can include more. A résumé should include the following:

- Your name in large font
- Your mailing address, phone number, and email address
- Bold headings and minimal white space
- Your previous and current education, including your major and GPA (if above 3.0)
- Your achievements and volunteer experience
- A summary of your qualifications or skills that are applicable to the desired position
- Your work experience, using action verbs & well-crafted descriptions that demonstrate your responsibilities and their values

- Example: Replace "I was only a cashier" with "Helped customers complete purchases, locate items, and join rewards programs to promote loyalty, satisfaction, and sales numbers."

Taking a Break?

Even with all the benefits of being a student-athlete at Miami, I still felt stress beyond what I originally imagined. During the winter break, I expressed to my father that I was considering taking a year off or quitting so I could make money and find what I truly wanted to do. College track workouts were much more demanding than high school track workouts, and my true love was still basketball. I am grateful that my father pushed me to continue because he realized that most students who take a break never return. He told me to look at my family members who did not finish college and determine if they were doing what they loved. He explained how college was not meant to be easy, and that finishing it through would be worth the struggle. Thanks Dad!

Freshman Year: Spring Semester

February of my first year was when my first college track seasons began! Thanks to being a student-athlete, I traveled across the country for free! This was my first time having an indoor track season and competing outside of Ohio. Interestingly around this same time, I requested a release so I could take an official visit to The Ohio State University with hopes of possibly joining their track team. This was largely due to Miami's Athletic Department making plans to cut funds from the men's track program and fire the coach who recruited me. This would mean I would not be able to earn a partial scholarship for future years. My coach and I had a tight bond, and he was one of the main reasons I attended Miami. He saw the talent in me, and we did not want it to be wasted by his potential replacement. The coach who was set to replace my coach called me into his office for a meeting. He almost came to tears expressing his desire for me to stay. An emotionally led person might cling to this, but I lead with logic. I heard from many athletes how he ran his team into the ground, meaning he overtrained them. Overtraining is something all athletes should avoid because balance is key in all aspects of life!

As I expressed my wants and thoughts to the Athletic Department, I realized something: "I AM THE PRIZE!" I checked all their boxes. I was a marginalized student, I was highly articulate, I had a high GPA, and I produced top-tier athletic results. With all of these ingredients, Miami certainly did not want me to leave. As I visited The Ohio State University, they had everything an athlete could ask for! They offered me a guaranteed spot but informed me that there was no money available. This reality would put me in the same financial position I was in at Miami. My parents allowed me to choose where I eventually wanted to go. A couple of weeks went by, and I received a surprise email and phone call explaining how Miami magically found some athletic funds and offered them to me if I chose to stay.

Dear Kenny,

Know the power you hold, be patient, and be smart enough to make your own decisions!

Sincerely,

Kenny Glenn, Success Coach and Entrepreneur

Throughout the indoor and outdoor seasons, I continued to adjust to the new level of competition. I also knew that if my coach was going to get fired, I wanted to send him off with a stellar season! Although I did not initially believe I was fast, Coach Reynolds saw my potential and believed I could be a sprinter. He pushed me to run the 4x100 relay, and my first time doing so would be in my first outdoor meet at Wake Forest University.

I was nervous about being on the 4x100 relay, especially as the anchor leg. I did no sprinting events in high school because of fear! I chose to stay comfortable with winning in my jumping events. I did not think I was fast enough, and I did not want to lose and do so in front of my teammates just to hear them say "you got cooked." I had carried this same mindset into college, and I was extremely nervous!

During the actual race, to make sure I did not "get cooked," I took off too early for my teammate to pass me the baton. I had to slow down so he could get me the baton within the legal exchange zone. During this time, the sprinters on both sides of me got their batons before me and were ahead of me. When I finally got the baton, I ran the fastest I had ever run! I eventually passed my competitors and won the race! When I crossed the finish line, I looked both ways in complete shock. It all happened so quickly that I do not even think I took a breath. This occurrence grew my self-belief, and afterward, I told my coach I wanted to stay on the 4x100 relay and even do the 100m dash!

My confidence grew with each meet, and I noticed my ability to compete with the best of the best! With the addition of my new sprinting events, I continued to get stronger and faster. At the age of 17, this new confidence, speed and strength helped me to achieve a long jump mark of 24 feet, 5 inches! This was a personal best, and it placed me on the list of top ten long jumpers in Miami history. That same jump also earned me a guaranteed spot in the first round of the National Championships in Jacksonville Florida.

This was a great way to end my freshman year and earn my very first plane ride!

Sophomore Year: Academics

As a sophomore, I felt much more comfortable as I established a routine that made academics and athletics easier to juggle. However, this is also the year I was officially admitted into Farmer School of Business. I had to increase the time I spent on homework for business classes, which led me to give up playing video games. Around this time, I was often asked, "Kenny, why do you go so hard?" The question would come from classmates and teammates when I would reject drugs or choose to study instead of following the crowd. I went hard because I saw so many people I grew up with who HAD IT! They had the opportunity to be star students or athletes, go to college for free, graduate college, and then change their family's lives for generations to come. But instead, they chose the comfortable path of giving up and making dumb decisions. Of course, I had fun and partied on occasion, but I always stayed focused on the bigger picture. Most people in our society want to feel good and be rewarded immediately, but I am here to tell you the importance of delayed gratification. This is the ability to postpone immediate pleasure in exchange for a greater reward that will come later. Delayed gratification can be applied in all areas of life.

Remember the story about me selling Starburst in the eighth grade? College taught me the "fancy" words for the concepts that I already knew. As you elevate throughout life, each new level will require a new language. Not language, as in French, Spanish, or German. The language I am referring to is when you must learn and use certain words or phrases to show your understanding of a subject. Business is simple, but the terminology can make it confusing to some.

Here is an example of an accounting breakdown: My mother drove me to the store to pick up my candy products. For a large-scale business, this would be considered shipping and freight costs. I then purchased inventory at a certain price, which was my cost of goods sold. I then sold those products to receive revenue. The money I was left with after I calculated the expenses was my gross profit. If I had to pay taxes, whatever I had left was my net income. I could reinvest that net income into growing the company OR I could pay myself. Use this example and terminology to help you better understand business fundamentals.

Sophomore Year: Athletics

This same year, I had come to terms with the fact I would be getting a new track coach. Russell Peterson, the new coach, would become a great friend. He is a young White guy, but it is obvious that he grew up in Black neighborhoods. His background and seeing my potential to be legendary helped grow our bond.

Coach Peterson made his presence felt around the athletic community when he invited a nutritional specialist to come speak on campus. This speaker explained the proper amounts of sleep we should get, what we should eat, and the harmful effects of drugs and alcohol. He stated and proved how getting intoxicated from alcohol causes an athlete to lose two weeks' worth of training. That day I chose to stop drinking alcohol during training because I could not afford the risk of throwing away the hard work I put in! These types of careless decisions are what negatively affect many college and professional athletic performances.

Around the same time, I still made a bad decision by choosing to play in an unnecessary intramural basketball game. I should have been out there just having fun, but I allowed my emotions to get the best of me. I was invited by my friend and classmate, Ahmad Peterkin. I played and lost against Ahmad and his school in my final high school basketball game. I was still hurt by this and had a chip on my shoulder from it. Even though I had not played basketball in months, I wanted to prove I was still a beast on the court! The team we went against began to play super hard. So I upped my intensity and played angrily. Then, in one play, I went for a rebound and came down on someone's foot. I felt my right ankle twist and thought it was a normal sprain. However, when I tried to get up and jog, I could not apply any pressure on it. I stayed for the rest of the game and then hopped on my good foot to my dorm next door. When I took off my shoe, my ankle immediately swelled up into what looked like three times its normal size! The pain was so unbearable that I could not even sleep.

It is a blessing that I did not break it, but the healing process was a long 13 weeks before I could sprint again. Then, I returned to sprinting too early and injured my left hip flexor because my body was overcompensating. I rushed back because I had something to prove! No matter what, I knew I was still the best athlete on the team, and I had to show my new coach how great I truly was! I also wanted to win a conference medal and return to the National Championships. The season was a struggle, all the way up until my last jump at the Conference Championships. The crowd was going crazy as the long jumpers from the University of Akron were about to win all three medals!

My teammate Pete Stefanski told me, "You better not let these guys sweep the podium!" I felt a bruise on my left heel from all the pounding I had placed on it from jumping and heavily relying

140

on my left leg. But I could not let that stop me in the moment! I mustered up everything inside of me as I sprinted towards the sand, and when I jumped, my only thought was, "Don't land! Don't land! Don't land!" Eventually, I did land and knew it was a massive jump. The measurement judges said out loud, "7.63 meters!" I screamed, "LET'S GOOOO!" while my teammates went wild with celebration as we knew this translated to 25 feet! This jump was a school record and guaranteed me a medal and a spot at the first round of the National Championships in Jacksonville, Florida again!

I cried tears of joy and redemption. Thanks to my young age of 18, this same jump qualified me for USATF Junior National Championships in Clovis, California. This competition was my first trip to the West Coast, and it was completely paid for. I saw and competed against current Olympians and World Champions like Noah Lyles and Grant Holloway.

CHAPTER 11

My Junior Year

My junior year provides another example that showcases the importance of networking, acting as if you belong, and not caring about the opinions of others.

The weekend before my junior year began, I paid $180 to see and hear Dr. Eric Thomas—more famously known as ET, the Hip Hop Preacher—give a speech in Indianapolis, Indiana. The event was only a 90-minute drive, and ET was the man I listened to every day on my quest to make my high school basketball team. Although I was a top-tier collegiate athlete, I was not as successful as I wanted to be in other life endeavors. I was so hype to see ET that I arrived an hour before the session I paid for was scheduled to start. During this idle time, I just so happened to waltz into the VIP session which had just ended. This was the room of people who spent $1,000 to have a private and catered session with ET. As I walked around the room, I was treated as if I fully belonged. So what did I do? I went with the flow and eventually shook ET's hand!

Afterward, I met and spoke with an audience member named Shareef Martin. Shareef introduced himself as a personal fitness trainer and brand owner who lived in Cincinnati, Ohio. Our conversation and synergies led to him gifting me with his event

VIP wristband. This allowed me to sit in the very front of the main speaking session. Weeks later, I visited Shareef's studio, and he gave me one of his branded shirts while also letting me train at his facility! Now back to the story.

When I arrived back home in Cincinnati, my family laughed at me and sarcastically said things like, "So you paid almost $200 to go listen to a guy talk?" I reacted like the typical teenager by getting upset and leaving. My father noticed this and called me to vocalize that they were just playing. He also said that if going to hear ET speak would help me accomplish my goals, then it was well worth it and that it does not matter what anyone else thought.

My First Apartment

Miami University has a money-grabbing rule that students must live in dorms on campus for their first two years. My junior year is when I was allowed to move off-campus. I found an apartment with four bedrooms and only one bathroom, but rent was only $1,250 per occupant per semester. This was a great find in terms of saving money, but in hindsight, it was not worth the stress! I picked the absolute worst housemates ever! I lived with three football players, and I am only still friends with two of them now. The one I no longer interact with was an annoying cancer. All he did was smoke weed, play video games, and depend on his mom to pay his portion of the bills! The constant trashing and smell of weed drove me insane.

I learned the hard lesson that just because people are your friends does not mean you should live with them. The stress I endured trickled over into the crumbling of my romantic relationship at the time. It also affected my body and athletic performance as I gained weight, lost speed, and racked up on injuries. My heightened level of stress and injuries led to my coach and me deciding to use the option of athletically redshirting my junior year. This option meant I would not travel or participate in competitions with the team during my junior year, but I would still have two more years of eligibility afterwards.

Dear Kenny,

On the journey of achieving what you want, there are habits, things, and people you will have to cut off. It sounds harsh, but it is necessary. Some people are unwilling to change, no matter how much you plead with them.

How do you know when to cut something off? If anything or anyone gets in the way or takes time away from what you need to do to get what you want. It may or may not have to get cut off 100% or forever. Sometimes these things, habits, and people must be put on a strict limit so they do not take away from your precious energy, time, and money.

For example, the reason I cut off my braids at age 12 was that getting my hair done took time from playing basketball on the weekends. One reason I am not fluent in Spanish is that I used the time I could have been inside the house learning from my mother to instead be outside practicing my basketball skills. More than anything else, I wanted to be on the basketball team. So I sacrificed wherever it was feasible to achieve my goal. I have even cut ties with women in romantic relationships because of the time and energy they would take away from achieving my goals.

Sincerely,

Kenny Glenn, Success Coach and Entrepreneur

Trauma, Fear, and Emotions

There was a time when therapy had the stigma of only psychopaths and serial killers using and needing it. Reluctantly, therapy services have become more accepted and commonly used by the general population. The reality is we all have experienced some level of trauma in our childhood and adulthood. Also, we each encounter highly stressful situations throughout our lives. The specific topic of trauma is still not talked about enough. Trauma is the response to any deeply distressing or disturbing event that disrupts one's central nervous system. When high levels of stress or mental trauma are not properly released or dealt with, they remain in the mind and body while leading to unhealthy coping mechanisms. This can occur by way of self-sabotage or the abuse of others, whether it is verbally, emotionally, or physically. Examples of this are compulsive unnecessary spending, excessive eating or sleeping, alcohol and drug addictions to "take the pain away," and sexual yet toxic relationships. These each bring feelings of temporary pleasure but cause more harm than good.

After many failed romantic relationships, I was forced to reflect on my childhood and certain destructive behaviors. My reflection and vocalization of past situations has allowed me to heal from past trauma, overcome fears, and release old emotions of anger and sadness. Before these helpful changes, I was short-tempered and reactionary. After one of my breakups, I felt so sad and depressed that I went to the store and took pictures of Hallmark cards to cheer myself up. Fortunately, since then, I have received direct and indirect help from therapists and psychologists. The direct help came from actual one-to-one private conversations. The indirect help comes from being around friends who have similar experiences and listening to how they persevered in a healthy manner. I also listened to celebrity interviews about how they used therapy and the perspectives they gained from the experience. They each talk about the importance of patience, breathing, positive self-talk, visualization, and body language.

Through reflection, I also noticed my tendency to push myself and others to be extremists by immediately giving up bad habits without relapse. The greatest lesson I learned is to be patient with myself and with others. Balance is necessary when expressing patience. Although patience is not an excuse to be lazy, change is easier when it is not rushed or overly forced. I also learned to not waste time trying to change or convince those who want to remain the same or move at their own pace. It is vitally important to always work on yourself first and be the living example others have the option to learn from.

Dear Kenny,

Take your mental health seriously and speak to someone about what is occurring in your mind. I know you spend lots of time earning money or strengthening your body, but your mental health is just as important. If you are in high school, speak with your school counselors and ask if they know of any free therapy services. As a high school graduate, use Google to find therapists, especially ones you can afford or those who accept your insurance. If you are in college, take advantage of the fact that most campuses offer FREE therapy services!

I understand that many students and graduates grow up in households that lack proper guidance or ideal relationship examples from parental figures. Yet, even in seemingly perfect scenarios, students may still witness certain things which negatively scar their subconscious minds and future behavior. This has a major effect on their reality and life perspectives. By reading this, you must realize you now have the power to choose how you respond to the trauma that has occurred in your life. Will you choose to leave it untamed and continue to control you? Or will you choose to heal and learn from it?

There are some people who hurt me, and I hurt them, in a non-physical way. This is in terms of emotions and feelings due to certain actions and words spoken out of anger and ignorance. I have forgiven those who have wronged me, and I have apologized to those whom I have wronged. My advice here is to heighten your emotional intelligence so you learn how to respond properly instead of reacting immaturely.

Shoutout to the late but great platinum recording artist Whitney Houston! She had her personal struggles, just like we all do, but she had an amazing voice. The song of hers that I will highlight is entitled "The Greatest Love of All." I recommend that you listen to the entire song and read the lyrics from a reputable source. I want you to focus on and internalize a specific line: "Learning to love yourself is the greatest love of all."

Fear is a natural human thought and reaction, but it should not be the sole or primary force which governs most of our lives and decisions. Ironically, people are afraid to even admit fear is what controls them. Some of the things most of us are afraid of are silence, being alone, public speaking, humiliation, hair loss, and death. In reference to silence and being alone, we fear these things because we relate them to feeling unloved or unwanted. It is okay to be afraid, but this is where courage is necessary to push through the fear. By being courageous and not letting fear stop you, you can become the positive individual you were truly created to be. Those around you will take notice and eventually decide to be courageous for themselves.

Here, I will reference the poem by Marianne Williamson entitled "Our Deepest Fear," which a character partially quotes in the movie *Coach Carter*. The first two lines are *"Our deepest fear is not that we are inadequate. Our deepest fear is that we are powerful beyond measure."* I want you to find this poem, read it out loud, and feel the vibrations of the impactful words!

Dear Kenny,

Unapologetically shine your light! This is what you were created to do! By doing so, you will serve as a spark and other people will begin to see the light in themselves.

Sincerely,

Kenny Glenn, Success Coach and Entrepreneur

The Value of Internships

An internship provides:

✓ An opportunity to apply what you have learned in the classroom.

✓ Real on-the-job training, practical experience, and marketability.

✓ Networking with experienced interns and associates at the company while gaining professional feedback.

✓ An opportunity to increase your professionalism and learn how to conduct yourself in an office setting and at company events.

✓ A chance to build your résumé and a better chance to gain future employment.

✓ An opportunity to figure out what you like and do not like about a specific profession!

I mentioned earlier in the book that I got rejected by my dream internship in California. Here, I will elaborate on the scenario. One of my goals for junior year was to obtain an internship, specifically with one of the "Big Four" accounting firms, Ernst & Young in San Diego, California. Big Four accounting firms were held in high regard at Miami University and heavily pushed on all business majors. My rejection news came via email shortly after returning to campus after my all-expenses-paid trip for the interviews. I had also told everyone I knew about the opportunity, and everyone agreed that I was essentially guaranteed the position. I was crushed by the rejection because of how badly I wanted the internship, and I knew I would face public embarrassment. I am grateful that my mother advised me to figure out why I was rejected and to move in silence by keeping certain plans quiet.

I asked the interviewers for reasons why I was rejected, and I opted to improve on each aspect. They informed me that I was not chosen for the internship because I did not ask the right questions or show them what they wanted to see. They wanted to see higher grades but also proof that I was truly interested in the field of accounting. I also personally reflected on areas where I could have been better. From a professionalism standpoint, I had no idea what I was getting myself into as I even took a picture of my plate during lunch. It might have been appropriate in a social setting, but an internship committee member might have found it inappropriate in a professional setting. Now, I know that every move I make in a professional setting is being watched and judged. I might have also looked like a "kid" who had never "been anywhere." I should have behaved as if I had been in that type of situation before, even though I truly had not.

The week after my rejection, I joined the National Association of Black Accountants (NABA), which allowed me to learn more about the accounting profession from students and graduates who looked like me. A mentor and campus co-founder of the Miami chapter of NABA, Leah Phillips, had previously asked me to join, but I told her I was too busy. It is funny how quickly that changed after my internship rejection.

Dear Kenny,

People will make time for what is important and needed to get what they desire. Dealing with rejection in any area of life can be difficult, but it teaches you how to be better. Ask yourself, "Is what I am trying to obtain or enter truly worth it?" If it is worth it, then ask, "How can I minimize my chances of getting rejected? Do I need more money? More experience? More confidence? More information?"

If you truly want it, figure out what you need and get to work! Still, you must also realize that not everything or every person is for you and that you are not for everything or every person. This is a true statement for opportunities as well. Be able to let go, be grateful for what you have, and find where you fit in best. Do not take things too personally. I know anger may arise when things do not go your way or you feel that someone has wronged you. However, there is no one out here with a personal vendetta or mission to make you miserable or ensure that you fail. Dust your shoulders off, grow from every experience, and continue to move forward. All success starts with you!

Sincerely,

Kenny Glenn, Success Coach and Entrepreneur

While in pursuit of obtaining my goal of solidifying a summer internship, I took the time to do a mock interview, as it was required for one of my business classes. During the mock interview, I was told I did well but needed to be less "humble" and quiet about my successes. This is where I give you one of the greatest lessons I ever learned:

Dear Kenny,

People will misuse and abuse the word "humble" to limit you if you let them. Certain individuals might ask you to be "humbler" when they hear you talk about your greatness or positive expectations. But when selling yourself in an interview or selling a product or service, you must courageously and confidently state why you are the best.

I always challenge people with this question: "So it's okay to be super confident in my mind, but soon as I vocalize how confident I am, now I'm suddenly not humble?" That sounds goofy when it is said aloud. When you vocalize how great you are, be sure to back it up as best as you can. If you fail, oh well, that's life. Get back up and try again.

In my opinion, the word humble is popularly or connotatively used as, "Do not vocalize your confident self-beliefs." When people say things like "They are too cocky" or "They need to be humble" what they are really saying is "They are too confident or too loud for my liking." If you Google search "humble," it is defined as "having or showing a low estimate of one's own importance." There are situations when you should lower your importance but not when you are competing, selling yourself as the best, or reassuring your self-esteem. I am not saying to overly brag and be obnoxious, but

151

know your worth, and recognize that the word "humble" is not synonymous with "quiet!" Ask people what they truly mean when they use the word humble. Do not allow the fear of being labeled "cocky" to limit your level of self-confidence. Before anyone achieved anything, they needed to think that they could achieve it.

Shoutout to Ben Phillips as he agrees with me on the point of there is no such thing as cocky. In my vocabulary and thought process, there is only confidence, doubt, delusion, and deceit. Confidence is to believe in yourself, and it grows with practice and repetition. Doubt is uncertainty or the lack of belief, the opposite of confidence. Delusion is to believe you are better or worse than you truly are. Deceit is inherently knowing the truth but outwardly expressing the opposite.

I have grown my self-belief to a level where I believe I can be, do, and have anything I set my mind to. This level of belief has turned into knowing myself on a deeper level and knowing my infinite abilities. Whether someone else agrees with me or not is not a concern of mine. Do your best to not let the opinions of others downplay you, your beliefs, or your self-esteem. In the words of the illustrious Deion Sanders, aka Prime Time or Coach Prime, "Do not allow my confidence to offend your insecurities."

Sincerely,

Kenny Glenn, Success Coach and Entrepreneur

Leah Phillips previously had an internship with KPMG, which is another Big Four accounting firm, and she still had a solid relationship with their recruiters. She kindly introduced me to them, which allowed me to meet them in person on the morning of the career fair. Our meeting was scheduled to occur at Starbucks, which was an informal setting and much less crowded than a career fair. Let me explain what a career fair is. It is a monstrous gathering of businesses and eager college students handing out résumés in hopes of scheduling job or internship interviews. Imagine thousands of people in suits and blouses packed into one area with Black Friday lines and tons of conversations happening at once. The power of avoiding that scenario was that the KPMG recruiters would be more likely to remember me. I would be the very first student they interacted with before speaking with hundreds of others throughout the day.

The night prior to the meeting, thanks to Glenn Trepeta, I wrote and reviewed a list of questions in my padfolio to ask the recruiters. I am not a coffee fan, and I had never been to Starbucks. Before they closed for the day, I visited Starbucks to ask employees what I should order. They advised me to order a chai tea latte and even let me sample it. I also had multiple copies of my résumé printed out because I knew the recruiters would ask to see it. I prepared as much as I could and then got some sleep.

I came to the meeting with a smile on my face and dressed in business casual attire. The first two questions were "What do you want to drink?" and "May I see your résumé?" After the recruiter ordered our drinks and scanned my resume, she comically asked, "When do you sleep?"

Her reason for asking stemmed from having an impressive and clear outline of the activities and organizations I was involved in, especially NABA. My resume showcased my ability to juggle responsibilities while also showing my interest in accounting. This was much better than when I interviewed with Ernst & Young a few months prior. As a student-athlete and business major, it is a question I just chuckled at. The real answer was that I made sure to get my seven to eight hours of sleep because I prioritized!

Her next question was "Do you have any questions for me?" This is when I knew that it was time to shine! I had the questions written down in my padfolio. If I had no questions, our meeting would have only lasted 5 minutes, and she probably would have chosen someone else to interview for the internship. Because I had those questions, it lasted closer to 40 minutes. I had failed in this part of the interviews before, and I made sure that would never happen again!

At the end of our meeting, she was impressed and then asked if I had any more questions. I looked at my notes and realized that I had already asked all of them thanks to memorization. They swiftly moved me into the next phase of obtaining the internship because of my resources and efforts. Thanks to being properly prepared, I decreased my chances of getting rejected!

Highly Effective Interview Questions

The questions I will list in this section work wonders, and I offer them to all readers to use and make their own. Some of them were given to me by my mentor and Miami alum, Glenn Trepeta. My mentees and younger sister, Nahja, have also used them to impress their interviewers and obtain internships and jobs.

1. What characteristics are you seeking in an ideal candidate?
2. As an intern, what are some ways I can add value to a client engagement?
3. What are some challenges that interns face when entering this role?
4. What changes in the profession, as well as this specific company, have you seen during your career?
5. If I were to randomly select people in the firm, what traits do you think would best describe them?
6. What are some things I can do now to hit the ground running if I am selected?
7. What do you enjoy and dislike when dealing with a client?
8. BONUS: If you could write a letter to your younger self, what advice would you give?

9. BONUS: Would you be opposed to scheduling coffee or lunch sometime so we can grow our relationship outside of this interview setting?

Dear Kenny,

Proper preparation is critical to achieving your goals! Write them down and intently focus on them. You can write them every day or write them once and put them somewhere you will see them every day. A great tip I used in college was putting my goal as my phone password. This forced me to think about and type in my goal at least 30 times a day! I wanted to jump 25 feet, and that is exactly what I eventually jumped. I wrote down the internship and travel opportunities I wanted to receive. Then, I went to work to make sure they happened! I did not achieve every single one of my goals, but I came very close. Some goals I even surpassed! Also, realize that your goals may change, but this is not an excuse to not write them down or procrastinate on achieving them.

Sincerely,

Kenny Glenn, Success Coach and Entrepreneur

After taking a family trip to Atlanta, Georgia, I no longer wanted to intern in San Diego, California. I shifted my goal thanks to the experiences and conversations I had with my cousin Shaquille Tensley, who lived in Atlanta at the time. After impressing the lead recruiter in Cincinnati, she gladly introduced me to the lead recruiter in Atlanta. I was scheduled to interview in Atlanta during my spring break, which was perfect timing since I would have class or track meets during other weeks. I asked the Atlanta recruiter if I could fly in a week early to further acclimate myself to the new city. This was a bold ask, but my explanation made sense to them, and they agreed! My track teammate Zuri Davis and I were on the same flight, and her mom allowed me to stay at their house for the first couple of days of my trip. Zuri gave me a grand tour of the city and took me to all her favorite places.

For the final days of my trip, my cousin Stormee Johnson allowed me to sleep at her apartment, as she was a student at Agnes Scott College in Decatur, Georgia.

Those were the precursors to acquiring my first internship. Now, let us dive into the next stages. When I applied to the Atlanta office, I had to explain why I was choosing a city outside of my hometown. I chose to state that my reason was family. Most students would have said, "I just really like the city." That type of answer compared to family is laughable. Saying you are moving to a city because of family holds more weight in the employers' minds. It shows that you really want to be there and are more likely to stay long-term.

The night before the interview I went to Walmart and bought a brown watch for $12 and a brown leather padfolio for $10. My dress shoes were brown, and I knew how important details were.

During the interview, I was up against two other student applicants who attended the University of Georgia. Things seemed neck-and-neck until the last interview, which was panel style. The first question was about taxes, and I knew very little about them! Thanks to our seating arrangement, I was the last to respond, and this gave me enough time to think of an answer that would woo the interviewers. I let them know I was quite familiar with taxes because both of my parents worked for the IRS! Each of their heads perked up, and they thought I knew more about the subject than most.

Please note that jobs are going to teach you everything you need to know; all you must do is properly get your foot in the door.

A few weeks went by, and I received a voicemail from my Atlanta recruiter letting me know I was chosen for the internship! I joyfully called her back to accept the position! This was a huge weight lifted from my back as I direly wanted an internship that aligned with my major and future career! I also wanted it to be paid and give me opportunities to travel. I would be making $25 an hour and be flown to New York and California for FREE!

Dear Kenny,

You are being watched and judged at all times; this is true anytime you are in a public setting. Be sure to control the narrative while also being your courageous self. You will be treated based on your actions, achievements, attire, and ability to articulate.

From an attire standpoint, you do not have to spend a lot of money to look wealthy. I bought my first neckties from Goodwill for $1 each! I learned how to tie those ties from watching videos on YouTube and practicing for 20 minutes. My father and I purchased all my suit jackets and slacks from JCPenney when they were on sale or on the clearance rack!

From an articulation standpoint, you may have to learn to speak formal English. It might seem unnatural at first, but this is not an example of "selling out." More appropriate ways to view it are "code-switching" and "buying in." How you speak, answer questions, and present ideas speak volumes about you. Study the successful people you want to be like.

One way to be perceived more positively is by wearing a suit to class, a restaurant, a shopping mall, or a sporting event. People will see your dapper appearance and mentally associate you with money and success. You will receive compliments and will be more likely to engage in high-level conversations. My college fraternity brothers and I chose to wear suits on campus every Thursday. Each time we did it, we turned many heads, and it honestly felt good to look good! We all form biases based on what we can detect with our five senses. Due to natural bias, when people see one person wearing a suit and another person wearing a tank top and sagging pants, they are highly likely to form two very different opinions on the backgrounds and careers of those persons.

You may not be someone who talks constantly or loudly, but when you do talk, make sure you are heard! There are certain environments or situations where it is necessary to talk more, and there are certain people with whom you should talk more. The opposite is true as well. Listening with intent is just as important.

Sincerely, Kenny Glenn, Success Coach and Entrepreneur

Graduate School Acceptance

This is an area where once again, my mentor Leah Phillips was instrumental during my college journey. I knew that Leah was in the Master of Accountancy (MAcc) program and that she was the only Black person in the program. This was an opportunity for me to take advantage of as well! I knew they wanted and needed more Black students in the MAcc program, especially Black student-athletes like me! In the spring semester of my junior year, I decided to apply for the Master of Accountancy program. I had the personality and gift of gab to speak with those in charge of accepting students into the program, and I had the undergraduate grades to get me in. Leah was a huge advocate and she helped me write my application essay. All these factors combined helped me to get accepted into the graduate program only 48 hours later. The funny thing is, I jokingly stated this would happen on a Snapchat video I privately recorded. My acceptance allowed me to earn dual credits towards both my undergraduate and graduate degrees, which would grant me the opportunity to earn my bachelor's and master's degrees in accounting at the same time.

I knew I would need an extra year, whether I earned my master's degree or not. Thankfully, degrees do not have dates. This means if it takes a college student 4 years or 6 years to graduate, the degree only signifies completion, not how long it took to achieve it. My situation was due to my number of credits, and the fact I had another year of track & field eligibility. From juggling both academics and athletics, there were some semesters when it was not feasible to take more than 12 or 15 credit hours. To be on pace to graduate from Miami University in four years, a student needs a total of 128 credit hours. This equates to an average of 16 credit hours per semester for a four-year span. For me to catch up in credits, I had to take summer courses and a winter course. I paid for them directly out of my pocket.

My message to all readers is to understand that not all athletes are on full-ride athletic scholarships, especially if the sport is not football or basketball. Of course, I knew student-athletes who had full-ride scholarships and were able to have their summer or winter courses paid for. Was I slightly jealous? Yes! But I was not jealous of their strenuous schedule and lack of freedom during their college tenure. They did not have a "free ride" as some people like to label it. The better label was "work-study" due to all the demands they had to withstand.

My Internship Experiences

I did not complete much meaningful work in my internship, but I did earn close to $5,000 in eight weeks. The experience was more about getting to know the culture and the people within the company. I spent most days going to lunch with associates and partners of the firm, all charged on the company's credit card.

I worked with three other interns in the Atlanta office, and they also had no idea what we were hired to do. Eventually, we figured it out while creating some funny memories. For intern training, the company flew each of us to New Jersey, about 30 minutes away from New York City. This is where we met with over 200 other Black and Brown interns from around the country. I am still friends with some of them today!

One of the closest friends I made at that training was Brandon Hardy aka B Hardy! He was only a freshman in college, but he had swagger, charisma, and an Atlanta accent that made him sound just like the comedian Chris Tucker. Brandon is a confident genius who wore a bow tie every day, and he once had the goal of becoming President of the United States! His aura has a positive gravitational pull, which he uses to lift the spirits of others. His network is expansive because he can spark meaningful conversations with anyone! He is the youngest of his siblings from the slums of Atlanta. He recognized the negative temptations in his environment and knew he had to become the positive change he wanted to see! Therefore, he took school seriously enough to be rewarded with scholarship opportunities that enabled him to attend the highly prestigious University of Notre Dame. He is now a proud graduate and earns more than six figures per year as a top-tier technology salesman.

A few weeks after intern training, the company then flew me out to Los Angeles, California. On this trip, I reconnected with some fellow interns I met in New Jersey and new students who would be interning the following summer. Both trips also allowed me to visit family members I had not seen in years! I saw and stayed with aunts, uncles, and cousins who showered me with love and let me know how proud of me they were.

My first internship taught me that I did not want to live in Atlanta. Instead, I wanted to return home to Cincinnati. I saw the major benefits of working full-time in Cincinnati after college. I could live with my parents to save money, help my friends with their small businesses, and give back to my alma mater.

After my internship in Atlanta concluded, I stayed an extra week in hopes of connecting with Dwight Phillips, as Atlanta was his hometown and city of residence. Dwight Phillips is a long jump legend turned coach! He is the fifth-best long jumper of all time, a five-time world champion, and an Olympic gold medalist. I had met him once before during my freshman year of college at a track meet at the University of Kentucky. Before then, I had no clue who he was, but he gave me and other athletes some autographed batons. On these batons, he wrote his personal best jump of 28 feet, 8 inches. After I saw that, I immediately did more research on him. Fast forward to my junior year of college. I wanted his advice on how to become a better long jumper. I was confident enough to tweet him and he replied to my tweet with his phone number. Since he was out of the country at the time, our in-person meeting would have to wait. Regardless, I certainly enjoyed my experience in Atlanta that summer. Afterward, I drove back to Ohio to prepare for my "senior" year of college.

CHAPTER 12

My "Senior" Year

During the fall semester of my senior year, or what I should rather classify as my fourth year on campus, I was already focused on securing my internship for the next summer. I also wanted to continue to expand my mind and skillset beyond school. I began reading books about mindset and skill development, such as *The Champion's Mind: How Great Athletes Think, Train, and Thrive* by Jim Afremow.

Since I did not want to return to Atlanta for my next internship, I met with the Cincinnati recruiter of KPMG to explain my thoughts on returning home to do my next internship. I knew she would perk up because the Cincinnati office only had two Black employees. This is an example of me leveraging the color of my skin because I knew they were seeking to increase their office diversity. Combined with my previous experience the summer before and the connections I made, I was pretty much guaranteed the position. I still had to go through interviews, but these were easy for me now, especially with my slew of interview questions.

In the previous chapter, I listed a question that I think is perfect to ask at the end of an interview. Ask the interviewer, "Would you be opposed to scheduling coffee or lunch sometime so we can grow our relationship outside of this interview setting?" Their response will give you hints on if they will vouch for you to receive the position. Although I do not drink coffee, this is the most used tactic to schedule private time with professionals. The first time I asked this question, my interviewer pulled out her calendar at that exact moment to schedule our lunch. The second time I asked it, I combined it with relatability. The interviewer worked in Columbus, Ohio. I told him that my sister had just started college at The Ohio State University, and I asked if he would like to get coffee or lunch when I visit my sister. He agreed to grab lunch with me, and this is when I knew he would vouch for me to receive the internship offer.

The result I wanted came quickly. Forty-eight hours later, I received the offer to accept the internship in my hometown of Cincinnati, Ohio!

Experiences with Cultural Bias

During my second internship, I immediately noticed the cultural structure of the corporate American workforce, as out of 1,200 interns, only 80 of us were Black. This was vastly different than my first internship. I also experienced the negative but somewhat comical effects of being a Black American. While creating a playful skit that would include an actor portraying a thief, my incredibly "diverse" team (a Black woman, Asian man, White man, Indian woman, and White woman) looked at me in agreement and verbalized, "You would be the perfect thief." I immediately called out their biased ways of thinking! They attempted to use my track & field background as their reasoning, but I respectfully disagreed. We were demographically diverse, but they maintained their non-diverse negative biases based on mass media portrayal.

Another incident occurred while leaving lunch with a White male associate. I said, "See you later" to the Black chef at our client's location. My associate asked, "How do you know that guy?" I smiled and said he and my dad went to the same high school. It was true, but the real reason I knew him was that I had made an effort to speak with him every day. He was the only other Black man in the building out of the 300 people I saw daily. In the realm of athletics, I had a White teammate say my hairbrush was similar to a brush for horses. They did not realize the difference in our hair textures and how that statement could be offensive.

I mentioned earlier in the book how bias is natural and necessary as we each have obvious differences. Should everyone be treated fairly and with respect? ABSOLUTELY! We are all connected, as we each have the internal desire to be loved and to fulfill our basic human needs. We also want the right to freely express ourselves and continuously rise towards self-actualization on Maslow's Hierarchy of Needs. However, from an external and biological standpoint, let's not act like we are 100% the same. People of different heights and weights wear different sizes and types of clothes. People from different cultures and regional climates have different facial, hair, and skin features. Respect should not vary based on these factors, but these differences do create the need for diverse product offerings. Our ancestral traits are the cause for our varying nutritional needs, like optimal amounts of sun exposure or environmental food preferences. One group of people is not better or worse, just different.

Dear Kenny,

Not to be cliché, but I have Black friends who have skin colors across the entire spectrum. Contrary to popular belief, some of them get sunburn. I have Mexican and Indian friends who love Black hip-hop and rap musicians. Although I did grow up around many White people, when I got to college, I learned that some of them are cool to hang out with. Not every stereotype is true, but some of them make sense. However, do not allow negative media portrayals to tell your story or choose who you will become. Who you choose to be is up to you! Be the positive change you want to see in the world. Despite the barriers you may have to fight through and dismantle, always remember to love yourself, embrace being different, and find people who appreciate you for all that you are.

Sincerely,

Kenny Glenn, Success Coach and Entrepreneur

Greek?

Advice for College Students and Graduates: The number one rule when joining a Greek-letter social organization is discretion. If you are thinking about joining one of these organizations, it must be a tightly kept secret! Find one or two people within the fraternity or sorority and have private conversations with them about your interest. If you enter the process of joining, continue to keep it a secret until the outside world needs to know. I will also warn you that joining a fraternity or sorority turns you into an instant celebrity within your college community. Everything you do will be watched and judged at a heightened level. Make smart decisions!

In the spring semester of 2018, my line brother Jason Steele and I crossed the burning sands into the Kappa Delta Chapter of Kappa Alpha Psi Fraternity, Incorporated. This was an amazing life achievement for both of us. Kappa Alpha Psi Fraternity, Inc. is a historically Black fraternity that was founded on the campus of Indiana University on January 5, 1911. The motto & fundamental purpose of the fraternity is "achievement in every field of human endeavor." I gravitated towards Kappa Alpha Psi specifically because of the motto, the way I saw brothers carry themselves, and the fact that two of my older cousins (Charles Harrington Jr. and Louis Johnson Jr.) joined in 1992 and 2008 respectively. Friends I grew up with—Blake Scott, Brian Pringle, and Jordan Lackey—also influenced my decision. The reason I chose to join while still an undergraduate at Miami was that I wanted to forever attach myself to something on and off campus that was historically Black. Even though I was an athlete on the track team, most of my teammates were White. I waited until later in my college career because I was so focused on being the best track athlete I could be. I also noticed two former track team-mates whose careers went downhill after they joined a fraternity, and I did not want that to be me.

Some of my close friends and family members joined different fraternities, but we still love and respect each other. We make funny jokes about our different organizations, but there is no malice behind our statements. However, I would be a hypocrite if I did not write about the cons of joining Greek life, whether it is a fraternity or sorority. I have witnessed friendships and romantic relationships break apart, even one of mine, due to new time con-straints that come with new responsibilities, jealousy, and the inability to handle the heightened attention. I have also seen physical fights between organizations and within the same organ-izations because of inflated egos and childish disagreements. Greek life is an example of any type of organization, as politics and pride will always be involved. If you choose to join or affiliate yourself with any group or organization, remember that you have your own brain and the ability to make your own decisions. This will help you to avoid being blindly sucked into the negative thoughts and actions that can stem from groupthink.

Dear Kenny,

Greek life can turn hostile in a flash, especially at parties. Focus on proper conflict resolution as there are better ways to resolve problems than physical violence by way of fistfights and guns. Ask yourself in any situation, "Am I responding based on logic or reacting based on emotions?

Sincerely,

Kenny Glenn, Success Coach and Entrepreneur

The Benefits of Joining Greek Organizations

Despite the negative occurrences, the positive benefits I have received continue to outweigh them! I am elated with my decision as I have gained lifelong brothers within my chapter, state, region, country, and across the entire globe! These connections allow me to fellowship with older and younger brothers within the fraternity to do and talk about anything! If I am in search of any type of profession—whether it be a stock trader, a high school principal, a lawyer, a psychologist, a department head for a university, or an international entertainment specialist—I only have to look within my chapter of Kappa Delta and find who I need. Each brother has an amazing story of how they continue to achieve, while also being willing to help others on their journey.

In this section, I will share real stories about me benefiting from such a tremendous brotherhood! These acts of love and money-saving opportunities would not be available to me if I had not joined Kappa Alpha Psi Fraternity, Incorporated.

I made one phone call to my fraternity brother Tray Carter, and in a 24-hour span, he picked me up from the airport in Atlanta, Georgia, gave me a professional haircut after his normal barbering hours, and let me borrow his car!

During my Olympic journey, I lived in Miami Florida for weekly stretches thanks to my chapter brother, the professional saxophone player Jon Ross, famously known as Jon Saxx. He lived in Miami and allowed me to stay at his house while we had some amazing conversations that inspired both of us. He is also from

Cincinnati, Ohio, and we have numerous background similarities and similar life perspectives.

While living in Atlanta, I only had to pay $100 for a king-size bed worth $3,000! I also had it delivered from Cincinnati to Atlanta at no extra charge, thanks to my chapter brother Rahshann Blackwell, the owner of Bolt Moving.

Words of Wisdom

During the process of joining a historically Black fraternity or sorority, prospective members learn and recite certain poems and wise sayings. I will highlight a wise saying entitled "Excuses," the poem "Invictus," & Frederick Douglass' speech about "struggle."

Excuses. From my knowledge, most historically black fraternities & sororities have adopted an adage about excuses. It reads:

> "Excuses are tools of the incompetent used to build worthless monuments of nothingness. Through excuses, things are seldom accomplished and never achieved."

To put it another way, excuses are useless in your pursuit of bettering your life or accomplishing tasks. If you truly want something, you must be courageous and unapologetic in your pursuit to go get it. When you do not do something, it is because you did not truly want it enough or see the importance of doing it.

Invictus. The last two lines of the poem "Invictus" by William Ernest Henley read as follows:

> "I am the master of my fate,
> I am the captain of my soul."

In other words, I AM IN CONTROL OF MY LIFE, AND I AM RESPONSIBLE FOR THE CHANGES THAT OCCUR. Anything you want—a healthy body, homeownership, college graduation, your dream job, or your true love—is up to YOU!

Struggle. One of the most significant lines from Frederick Douglass' speech entitled "West India Emancipation" (1857) reads as follows:

> "If there is no struggle, there is no progress."

This line should be self-explanatory, but I must dive deeper. I could give countless examples, but here, I will share a few of the most profound ones. If you want stronger muscles, you must train and tear them. By "tearing" muscles, I am referring to healthy muscle development through vigorous workouts—not preventable or debilitating injuries caused by recklessness or unnecessary straining. If you want to learn any subject or improve any skill, you must practice different problems and know that you will get some wrong during the process. A seed must burst to become the flower or tree it is destined to be. Your mother had to be patient for nine months and go through unimaginable pain to push you into this world. The point I am making here is that if something is truly worth achieving, you will endure some type of struggle.

Staying disciplined is an example of struggle. I am not writing this and pretending that I have completely mastered self-discipline, but I have implemented tactics and gone through phases of my life where increasing my self-discipline was required to grow. You must choose the pain of discipline or the pain of regret. Get a coach, a team, or friends, who are going to hold you accountable. For example, it is much easier to get to the gym at 5:00 AM when I know my friends, teammates, and coaches will be there to go through the struggle with me.

Being a Kappa man during my college career also taught me more about business, marketing, and politics. We created and hosted community service events as well as study sessions, and we provided on- and off-campus entertainment. It seemed like every Black student on campus would attend our parties because they were JAM PACKED! This was when I learned the valuable lesson that people would rather be entertained than educated. When we hosted a financial literacy event, few students attended. The reality is sad, but someone must shift the paradigm!

Ironically, in the same semester I entered Greek life, I eventually fell victim to the same distractions as my former teammates. My athletic performance suffered, and I started to believe the hype from people who attributed my past achievements to pure talent. The true and overwhelming factor of my success was the consistent time, energy, and focus I had put into being a great athlete. I began placing more focus on Greek life and was too busy trying to be cool and look good instead of being good and looking cool! I had a horrible track season, and it was the first time in my college career, I did not improve my personal best or qualify for the National Championships. As I reevaluated what was important for my legacy, I knew I would have to redeem myself in my next and final season. One of my accounting classes during this semester gave me a dual credit opportunity. I failed one of the exams, which caused me to earn a C in the course. The C put me in danger of being kicked out of the program because it caused my graduate school GPA to start at 2.0. I would need to lift this to above a 3.0 with my future graduate courses to complete graduate school.

Meeting a Legend

I learned of J.C. Baker, now Dr. J.C. Baker, thanks to Ali Barnes. I met Ali at Miami University while he was a fellow student-athlete on the basketball team. Some students and athletes labeled Ali as an oddball because he thought beyond his playing days while also enjoying the college party scene. His own teammates mocked his genius idea of futuristic training methods. He invented Hip Hop Handles, which is now known as ProElite Training. Today, ProElite Training is a trademarked patent and mobile platform which helps train athletes with the metronomes of music to increase rhythm, pace, and tempo. I resonated with this idea because it was simple and made perfect sense. In addition, I loved the game of basketball, but my ball-handling skills needed some improvement. I knew this concept would help me & many others.

Through Snapchat stories, I noticed Ali would constantly talk about Dr. J.C. Baker and the amazing things they were working on in the technology, sports, and entertainment industries through business consulting. My interest to be a part of this greatness continued to grow, and I wanted to learn more. Ali and I exchanged messages, and I let him know I supported him and wanted to eventually help in some way. The funny thing was, I was never able to identify who Dr. Baker was through pictures and videos if Ali even showed him on camera. Based on mental programming and how much Ali raved about him and his million-dollar business endeavors, I thought Dr. Baker was White.

In the summer of 2018, after my fourth year and during the beginning of my second internship, Ben Phillips and I conversed via text to confirm that we would attend a Black Achievers Event. This event was the first of its kind, as it was marketed to bring together Black professionals in the Greater Cincinnati region. At the actual event, Ben and I were the youngest men there by 20+

years. Near the end of a speed networking session, Ben told me he was ready to leave, but then a moderator announced, "Dr. J.C. Baker is next to speak." I tugged at Ben and said, "WE MUST STAY to hear this man speak, as I have heard too many great things about him." Hearing this announcement also confirmed that Dr. Baker was Black, and I would finally get to see him! This was during a time when I felt like I was dying on the inside whenever I showed up to my internship. The company tasked me with some of the most boring and pointless work. Many days, I would be at my cubicle hoping and praying to find someone Black to work for in terms of business, consulting, and innovative solutions. Meeting Dr. Baker was the answer to those prayers!

Dr. Baker spoke with so much authority and charisma about Black wealth, his books, and his company's involvement with high-level deals around the globe. He asked the audience, "How many Black billionaires were there last year?" Most of the audience had no idea but somehow, I knew the answer was three. The three were Oprah Winfrey, Robert Smith, and Michael Jordan. Dr. Baker then spoke on the fact that their combined wealth was $7 billion compared to Jeff Bezos alone being worth $132 billion. He talked about how important it is to get things done instead of just talking about them. Too many times people want to meet over and over again before an actual change or partnership occurs. Ben and I knew we had to be attached to whatever Dr. Baker was involved with. The event ended 10 minutes after his speech, and we immediately used this opportunity to shake hands and talk with Dr. Baker about potential opportunities.

Dr. Baker met with Ben and me on separate occasions to further explain the type of work he did and how we could fit in to help. Then, he gave us the opportunity to learn about true entrepreneurship, sit in on meetings, and eventually earn real dollars. He also invited us to his house to play basketball on the full-size court in his backyard on the Fourth of July. Of course, we accepted! Upon arriving at his house, I was in pure amazement! I had only seen this type of wealth on television shows that showcased the lives of celebrities. That same day also happened to be the second anniversary of Dr. Baker officially creating his company. So it was also a celebration of his freedom from the corporate world. No coincidence there!

Bet on Yourself

During my internship, and after meeting Dr. Baker, I knew I would eventually have to bet on myself. The following story about my first gambling experience inside a casino is fitting:

To celebrate my 21st birthday, my family took me out to eat at Hollywood Casino for their famous seafood buffet. Afterward, we went to the gambling part of the casino because it was the first time that I was allowed to enter. The first game I played was roulette. This game uses a spinning wheel with 37 numbered pockets in assorted colors. The wheel is spun one way, and a small ball is bounced around before it lands on a certain number and color. I had a feeling that it would land on the color black. So I placed $10 on black. My dad said I should have put my money on my lucky number 22, which is the equivalent of betting on myself to win. I asked what I would receive if I put my money on an exact number, and I vaguely remember someone in the crowd of people answering my question by saying, "the same thing." This placed me under the impression that I would win the same amount of money that I put down.

The dealer then drops the ball, it spins around the number wheel, it lands on my lucky number 22, and the color was black. I won $10! After I picked up my winnings, I asked the dealer how much the payout would be for betting on an exact number. The dealer told me it was 35 to 1, and my jaw hit the floor! That meant that if I had put my $10 on the number 22, I would have won $350 instead of $10. This was confirmation that I would always bet on myself and reject "playing it safe."

Upon graduating, I knew I wanted to work with Ali Barnes and Dr. Baker because of the potential to learn and earn my dollars in a meaningful way that aligned with my passions. KPMG in Cincinnati offered me a full-time position, and my parents wanted me to accept the position. However, something deep in my soul told me that working with Dr. Baker would be the best decision! I had no student loan debt and only one monthly bill, which was a $250 car payment. I knew more guaranteed money would come later, but I needed the entrepreneurial knowledge ASAP!

Ben and I also told our friends and classmates Rod Mills and Kyle Broadnax about the great opportunity Dr. Baker presented us with. They too decided to join in, but it was Ben who was the most involved at the beginning of this new relationship. As we entered the new school year, I chose not to participate in many of the available opportunities with Dr. Baker because I needed to earn a B or higher in every class of graduate school so I could graduate. Furthermore, my final collegiate track season was coming up, and I wanted to minimize all distractions.

Dear Kenny,

Although they are often used interchangeably, but there is a difference between "information" and "knowledge." Information is received through facts and perspectives. True knowledge is gained through personal experience. You might "know" something based on information or what someone told you, but you will not be truly knowledgeable until you have a personal experience. You will need both to achieve your definition of success.

Sincerely,

Kenny Glenn, Success Coach and Entrepreneur

CHAPTER 13

My Fifth and Final Year

To my surprise, graduate courses seemed easier than undergraduate courses. I say this because they cut out the fluff and increased the focus on the most relevant subject matter. It also seems easier because graduate students have matured and become more focused than they ever were before. However, there were still times when I struggled and needed help in certain courses. Thank God for Joaquin Garza! Joaquin graduated from my high school a year after me. We knew each other but not on a friend or "let's hang out" type of level. Later, he chose to attend Miami University and became a finance major. Having similar backgrounds and knowing that many from our high school did not have the same opportunities, we helped each other in any way we could. We inevitably made the decision to become housemates. Then, we were both accepted into the Master of Accountancy program and for KPMG internships in Cincinnati. Honestly, without Joaquin, I probably would not have completed graduate school on time. Joaquin also had an exclusive all-access parking pass for his car, which he would let me drive to class and track practice!

Questions We Must Ask Ourselves

I created these questions before my final collegiate track seasons. I will use athletic references, but they are still beneficial for students and graduates who do not participate in sports. Relate these questions and explanations in ways that are meaningful to your life. These three foundational questions are great starting points and will lead anyone to dig deeper.

1. Do I believe in myself?
2. Do I trust my coach or mentor?
3. How great do I truly want to be?

If athletes do not believe in themselves, it will show on the outside. They will look nervous and tense. On the inside, they will begin to worry about the thoughts of others instead of focusing on executing what they have practiced. My parents believed in me before I ever believed in myself. But to reach and maximize my potential, I had to fully believe in myself. If you read this and you feel like nobody believes in you, I BELIEVE IN YOU! Now pick your head up and use your power to make your dreams a reality!

If an athlete does not trust their coach, they will eventually use them as a scapegoat if they do not perform how they think they should. However, a coach cannot do the assigned activities for their athlete, such as running a race or shooting a ball, just like a teacher cannot take or pass a test for their student. Both can only provide guidance and wisdom. I doubt that a teacher would intentionally sabotage their students. However, since teachers do not know everything, they still suffer from ignorance. It is you who must take a hard look in the mirror. If you disagree with your coach, mentor, or teacher, it is your responsibility to have tough but respectful conversations with them about how you feel. Coaching, teaching, and mentoring are all two-way streets of communication. Communication is the giving and the receiving of information. Listen to your coach, teacher, or mentor and respectfully tell them what you are thinking and feeling.

Asking yourself how great you want to be allows for reflection and foresight. You are then led to think and ask, "Do my actions, decisions, habits, friend groups, and food intake concur with the level of greatness I say I want to achieve?" Find and maximize what helps and coincides with your goals. Decrease or eliminate what does not.

I accompany these questions with a letter I wrote during a business management class and shared with my teammates.

Dear Teammates,

Greatness is a choice. Coach or anyone else who tries to help you can only give you tips and tools so you can do and be better. But it all comes down to a choice to want to do the right things. You have to want to be great and work your tail off. Trust what the coach is saying and give it your all. "I can take you to the water, but I cannot make you drink."

You have to see the bigger picture. Everything you are doing now is preparing you for the future. Will your future self say "thank you" to your past self? If you are half-assing and giving lackluster effort, then don't get mad when you earn those same results.

Sincerely,

Kenny Glenn

Mr. Figure It Out

Before my last semester of college, the scholarship I received thanks to my father's former military involvement (which paid about 95% of my tuition) was abruptly taken away. The program noticed my graduate courses and disqualified me from receiving further financial assistance. My father explained to them my special situation of being in a combined undergraduate and graduate program, but there was no way of getting it back. My mother already knew I would figure it out, and that is exactly what I did.

I researched scholarships that Miami offered to graduate students, and sure enough, I found one that was specific to graduate students with marginalized backgrounds. It is rare for scholarships to be granted in the middle of a school year, but my situation was also rare. I spoke with the necessary staff members and explained my situation in a way that painted a picture of "I really want to stay at Miami, but without being granted this scholarship, I will have to transfer."

For my graduate program, this would mean they would have another graduating class without a Black student, and it would tarnish their diversity goals. I knew this and leveraged it! I was originally told they would do their best to find a scholarship if any more were available. You better believe they found the money to pay for me to stay and graduate from their program. This is another example of how I used my skin color as an advantage instead of a hindrance. I just had to be creative and willing to find whatever was necessary.

My Last Collegiate Track Seasons

Before my last seasons, I sought advice from a former teammate, Andrew Dusing. After a near 20-year stint, he was one of the first Miami track & field athletes to achieve All-American status. I asked him what his mindset was as he prepared for his final season. He explained to me that he started to believe that he was one of the best in the country, and that he should be one of the top three finishers in every competition. His advice was added confirmation to be confident in my abilities to achieve my big goals.

In these seasons, I also finally had a coach who was strictly dedicated to jumps! No offense to my coaches Chad Reynolds and Russell Peterson, but they are all-around coaches who had to split their time with the whole team. Coach Tyler Sunwall came in and only had his eyes on me and the other jumpers on our team. He helped to grow my confidence and knowledge in the event of the long jump. He was also open to my ideas of trying new cues and techniques. Our first couple of indoor meets together were shaky as we got adjusted to each other's styles during competition. But eventually, I had some big indoor jumps which allowed me to qualify for the USATF National Championships in New York. This was an opportunity to compete against professional athletes from around the country.

During my last indoor track season, I also had the opportunity to be flown out to Microsoft's headquarters in Seattle, Washington for a final interview thanks to Akosua Boadi-Agyemang. She lives BOLDLY and has even gone viral by doing so. She posted on LinkedIn about the struggles of obtaining an internship as an international student in the United States. This attracted the attention of millions, most importantly, recruiters and CEOs around the globe. Even though I wanted to work with Dr. Baker, he still supported my decision to interview with Microsoft. I originally accepted the opportunity for the final interview, and Microsoft paid for my flight and hotel. However, it came about that the USATF National Championships would be held on the same day, and Microsoft would not allow a makeup date. I chose track over Microsoft because it was a once-in-a-lifetime type of opportunity! The cost of this decision was giving up the preparation I had done to get the Microsoft position.

Being forced to choose one or the other because of a date conflict saddened me, but everything happens for a reason! If I had chosen to go to the Microsoft interview instead of the track championships in New York, I would not have switched my long jump technique to what I saw better jumpers doing. I also would not have reconnected with Ryan Billian, my former competitor-turned-friend and professional training partner. Ryan informed me about being a professional track athlete while also being coached by Dwight Phillips, the same coach I sought advice from after my first internship. I did not give much thought to becoming an Olympian or a professional athlete until that moment.

Additionally, I would not have the same experiences that led me to write this book, and fortunately, my interview preparation did not go to waste. I was able to gift everything I had learned to my good friend Adrian Awuah, which helped him attain a full-time position with Microsoft in the same program I had sought after. At the championships, I achieved fifth place and won $1,000! Unfortunately, as a college athlete in 2019, I was not allowed to accept the money.

In the first outdoor meet of the season, I implemented a new jumping technique and purposefully involved the crowd. This technique helped me jump a new personal best, breaking my previous collegiate school record! In the long jump, some jumpers will include a clap routine to involve the crowd which increases excitement and helps gain a rhythm. Until my last season, I was nervous about implementing this tactic because I did not want to draw too much attention to myself, only to fail. I had fearful thoughts such as, "What if I foul?" or "What if it's a bad jump?"

This time around, I turned that fear into fuel. I switched my thoughts and answered my own questions: "If I foul, then I will just jump again because it is not the end of the world. I will not have a bad jump because I have practiced way too many times to let that happen. All eyes will be on me, whether I use the clap or not, because I came here to win and be the best! I might as well give the crowd what they came to see while spreading the fun."

With my new coach, technique, and mindset shift, I felt like I was back in high school! I won or placed in the top five at every meet I traveled to. This included the prestigious Penn Relays, which seem as if the entire country of Jamaica comes to watch. Then, during a meet at Indiana University, I jumped a lifetime best of 7.80 meters, which translates to 25 feet, 7 and ¼ inches! Every centimeter counts. I have seen long jump competitions lost by one centimeter, including some of mine. I thank Treyton Harris for pushing me to jump so far that day. Treyton was an Indiana University long jumper whom I constantly saw and competed against at meets throughout my college career. Our battles helped us grow a mutual sense of respect and a solid friendship.

With this success as a student-athlete, I had constant opportunities to get better at public speaking and dealing with the media. Many times, I was interviewed with cameras directly in my face and no time to prepare. Even at the mature age of 21 and during my fifth year of college, I still imitated what I saw from big-time celebrities like Russell Westbrook. In one of my interviews, I decided to wear sunglasses indoors, and Coach Peterson was not a fan of this. He felt and expressed to me that such behavior was unprofessional and a poor reflection of his leadership. In my defense, I was just having fun and doing what I saw professional athletes do. This is an example of why I do not entirely place blame on students and graduates when they are simply imitating what they see from media icons. Someone who cares about them needs to show them a better way to present themselves professionally.

Graduation Time!

Even with my success on the track, I still had to work extra hard in the classroom. I was digging myself out of a GPA ditch. There was no time for parties, as I had to make sure I earned an A or a

B+ in each of my graduate courses. Some of my previous professors had lowered my grade due to low participation, which is typical of graduate-level coursework. Moving forward, I made sure I participated in class meaningfully and more consistently than anyone else. This type of focus allowed me to get A's on accounting exams, which is something I had never done before! Still, there was one class every student in the graduate program struggled with. I purposefully sat in the front of this class and established a solid relationship with my professor. Unfortunately, I did not do well enough on the final exam to solidify a B+ in the class. However, thanks to my participation throughout the entire semester, my professor gave me the grade I needed to graduate!

Dear Kenny,

Your college professors highly appreciate it when you participate and establish personal relationships with them. Do this and you will see the benefits!

Sincerely,

Kenny Glenn, Success Coach and Entrepreneur

It would have been embarrassing not to officially graduate because I had family from New York and California coming to Ohio to celebrate my accomplishments. I needed at least a 3.00 GPA, and thanks to my increased focus, I squeezed by with a 3.02. This guaranteed I would graduate and not need to attend another college course!

I also saved money at graduation time. I still owned my high school graduation cap and gown, which were black. Although Miami University's colors are red and white, master's graduates wear the color black on graduation day. This reality saved me $70, and I only had to buy a master's hood. I kept this hood and let my younger sister use it later for her master's graduation ceremonies.

Dear Kenny,

Once you achieve your degree, it does not matter how long it took you! You may have gotten some C's, but you outweighed them with A's and B's. What matters is that you completed what you started. Along the journey, you overcame every obstacle that was thrown your way. You connected with some fantastic people, and now you will join an illustrious group: the alumni. Utilize that title to your full advantage. You earned it, and now it is time to reap the benefits!

Sincerely,

Kenny Glenn, Success Coach and Entrepreneur

I am extremely grateful to have graduated with no college debt, thanks to my father's military veteran status and his willingness to pay portions of my tuition and housing. Earning academic and athletic scholarships provided tremendous assistance as well. This reality allowed me to accept an entrepreneurial position with Dr. Baker & Associates that had no hourly wage, salary, or monetary guarantees. After graduation, I would save money by living with my parents and only paying a $250 monthly car payment until I traded that car in to save even more money.

Although I have achieved my master's degree, my advice to anyone considering getting theirs is to think carefully about how they can leverage the degree. No matter how many master's degrees you are offered, **the greatest thing you can ever master is yourself.**

Also, graduating from college with no student loan debt is not the norm. I understand many graduates take whatever job offer they can find because of the debt they must pay. This occurs much too often, even if the job does not align with their passion. I see this in graduates who want to be full-time entrepreneurs, but sometimes patience is necessary. There is no shame in being an employee while also growing your side hustle to a level where it can eventually become your main source of income. My advice to those who find themselves in these types of situations is to do what they have to do until they can do what they want to do. If you have the guts to do otherwise, then do it! But recognize the risk you are taking.

SECTION 5: POST-COLLEGE WHIRLWIND

Absorb what is useful. Discard what is not.
Add what is uniquely your own.

— BRUCE LEE

CHAPTER 14

Graduated From College... Now What?

This chapter is about my immediate journey after graduating from college as well as what the typical graduate encounters. When college students become college graduates, they have the same "Options of E's" as high school graduates, just at a heightened level thanks to their college degree. As a reminder, those four options that start with the letter E are as follows: employment, enrollment, entrepreneurship, and enlistment. I know graduates who have made singular choices from these options, as well as various combinations.

Most graduates choose the employee route, as this is their opportunity to begin their working career and experience life without school. A graduate's first job after college is typically in the industry that aligns with their newly acquired degree. There is a chance they interned with the company prior to accepting a full-time role. Some graduates choose to expand their employment options by interviewing with multiple companies before and after graduation. After selecting an employer, most graduates choose to get their own apartment so they can keep the same level of freedom they obtained in college. I advise you to focus on more than just salary when choosing an employer. Work environment and benefits like health insurance and vacation days are important. Also, the days of staying with one company for 40 years are gone! You will probably stay with your first company for five years max, maybe even one or two years before moving on to something better. Even if you love the company you work with, always keep your options open.

Of course, some graduates choose to stay enrolled in school after achieving their bachelor's degree. Those who choose this option seem to have a solid plan of how they will leverage the higher level of schooling, or they have become institutionalized and cannot envision life without school. These types of graduates are seeking master's or doctoral degrees in specific subjects, such as law, business, or healthcare.

Some graduates start businesses and leverage the resources they gained from college. Graduates who have a strong sense of self-belief that they will become profitable business owners often go this route. This option also is chosen by graduates who want to earn extra money while working for an employer or continuing to be enrolled in school.

The last E is for enlisting in the military after graduating from college. Often, graduates choose this option to help pay off their student loans. In exchange for service to their country, the military offers opportunities to pay off loans more quickly than any other institution.

Regardless of what students and graduates decide, it will always be important to understand the benefits and risks of each choice. I would be a hypocrite if I did not advise you to find mentors and ask questions to help decipher and decide what is best for YOU! Ultimately, students and graduates must live with the consequences of their choices. I advise college graduates to read and apply the lessons and ideologies in the Financial Literacy chapter of this book.

You will probably be making more money than you ever have before. If you are the first in your family to graduate from college, you may become the person everyone asks to borrow money from. If you decide to lend money, consider it a gift because you may never see that money again. I learned this lesson the hard way multiple times. Also, it is typical that the more money we make, the more we spend. It would be wise to live below your means, regardless of your income. I am not saying you shouldn't buy and have nice things, but be conscious of your financial health. Does it make sense to get a luxurious apartment that forces you to live paycheck to paycheck?

Dear Kenny,

No matter what level of schooling you complete or how much time passes, mentors will always be important. You may even need to hire and pay them. You do not need to do or figure out everything by yourself. I could figure out how to build a house to save money, but it would cost me valuable time! If I hire house-building experts, they will accomplish the task much more quickly while I do something else. All the information and advice I have given is to help you become a great adult. Do not throw away the lessons once you become an adult.

Sincerely,

Kenny Glenn, Success Coach and Entrepreneur

My journey was not typical, but the lessons I learned can benefit all. I still had so much more to learn about life and about myself. It all came down like a ton of bricks, and I did not take ample time to relax or celebrate. Gratefully, Miami University gifted NABA members with an all-expenses-paid trip to Las Vegas for the NABA annual conference and 50th-year celebration.

Immediately afterwards, it was time to shift my focus towards business consulting as well as becoming a professional athlete and a school board member.

The Business Hospital

To earn money and gain knowledge, I began working with Dr. Baker and his company, Dr. Baker & Associates – The Business Hospital, formerly known as J.C. Baker & Associates. My title was Junior Consultant, and I was tasked with finding and soliciting potential clients who needed help with their businesses. I was and will always be passionate about small businesses. So this was the majority of my target audience. Since I am also Black, these were the business owners I spoke with the most. However, I still found and helped clients from all demographics.

I quickly learned that the race of the business owner, the size of the business, or the country the business operated in, did not matter, as they all faced similar problems. The type of problems I am referring to cannot be fixed with more money. We served clients across multiple industries such as apparel, fitness, technology, education, construction, medical, food & beverage, event planning, and even gold mining! Most of their problems consisted of weak internal controls, poor salesmanship, and the inability to clearly identify or articulate their value propositions.

When I first began soliciting, I contacted any and everyone who even looked like they had a business or business idea. I used multiple methods to contact people such as calls, texts, emails, and direct messages on social platforms. This included complete strangers and people I had not talked to in years. I also asked friends and family if they could introduce me to any business owners. An "old school" tactic that help me practice my salesmanship, grow my confidence, and increase actual conversion was when I would put FOOT TO PAVEMENT! I would physically walk up and down streets or within shopping plazas to introduce myself to business owners, learn about their businesses, and probe them about their pain points. Here are the biggest lessons I learned from this style of sales:

- It is a numbers game, and you will be told "NO" many more times than you are told "YES." Keep going and be persistent.
- You must have the confidence to say what needs to be said OUT LOUD.
- You must clearly articulate your value proposition and worthiness of receiving the sale. Let people know who you are, what you do, why you are the best at it, and why you should be paid your price.
- There are certain types of questions to ask to get anyone to engage in dialogue.
- Learn how to simultaneously listen to what people say AND what they do not say.
- Learn how to overcome objections and contradictory statements.

Dr. Baker and I would ride all around Cincinnati to different business engagements. These would be meetings with potential and current clients, as well as meetings at banks and various Chambers of Commerce. We would drive purposefully slowly to look around at the different businesses and ask questions like: "What is their product or service?" or "How have they remained in business after all these years?"

I did not go through this journey alone, as I also had my class-mates and friends, Benjamin Phillips and Rod Mills. They also worked as Junior Consultants, and we were all on the same mission. All of us were young and hungry salesmen trying to earn money at every chance while helping our business community. We did not know what we were doing, and many times it showed. Sometimes Dr. Baker had to verbally spazz out on us so we would learn the lesson of why we were rejected. On many occasions, Dr. Baker would say, "I bet you didn't ask them this..." to make us realize where we were falling short. Here is an example of the lessons he would teach us:

"The fun part of starting a business is the logo design, choosing colors, imagery, fonts, and creating a website. It is like kindergarten (arts & crafts, recess, lunch, and field trips). Novice business owners are not interested in the strategy, development, legal, risk, or organic revenue generation. Rarely anybody knows exactly what they are doing. Schools are filled with people with degrees, and they are still failing. Your physician, your dentist, your lawyer, and your psychologist all operate PRACTICES; meaning they do what they THINK is best but there is no 100% guarantee. We exist to improve the health of businesses and teach things that they do not know, which should be used to increase effectiveness and efficiency."

Dear Kenny,

The business lessons from Dr. Baker also apply to life! People say they want things like a healthy body that looks good and functions properly, low-stress relationships with beautiful people, first-class flights around the world, and nice homes, but many do not want to do what is necessary to achieve these freedoms. If you are not willing to take risks and give what is necessary to achieve what you desire, do you truly want it?

Sincerely,

Kenny Glenn, Success Coach and Entrepreneur

I received so much valuable information and gained applicable knowledge in such a short time frame after graduating from college. I spent four years in college business courses, and yet, I learned more about business in the first four weeks of working alongside Dr. Baker. I realized that in businesses with fewer than five employees, owners must wear every departmental hat. They are responsible for sales, marketing, bookkeeping, legalities, customer service, and more. It was fun learning, teaching, and performing all these aspects. My first clients were business owners I had known personally since I was a teenager, such as Matt Waters, owner of YAECO. It was incredibly rewarding, internally and financially, to be hired to help them with their businesses!

I also quickly realized how entrepreneurship is not all sunshine and rainbows, even for the person who is helping other entrepreneurs. I experienced some months when I did not make a dime! I would be on phone calls or in meetings for 16 hours a day just trying to close deals. I had clients who were on the same grind which eventually leads to major burnout. As a salesman, some people would say they would call me back or say they were ready to pay and hire me, but they never did. The difference between this role and an employee role is that I still would have received some type of hourly wage or salary as an employee. My employer also would have covered my healthcare insurance. With the choice of commission-only work, I had neither of these aspects and had to cover my own insurance to see my general health physician, dentist, and eye doctor.

When the COVID-19 pandemic arrived, our workload increased because businesses around the world had no clue what their next moves should be. This was the perfect time to be "The Business Hospital" as we offered treatment and beneficial advice for businesses to properly get through this unprecedented and unpredictable situation. It seemed as if I could not have found a better position for my post-graduate life, and it fit perfectly with

195

my other pursuits of being a professional athlete and a school board member.

My Journey to the 2020 Olympics

The thought of becoming a professional track athlete started with the conversation I had with my friend Ryan Billian during USATF National Championships in February 2019. Ryan told me he and other professional track athletes were being coached by Dwight Phillips in a group called the Winners Circle. I knew that having the opportunity to be coached by Dwight Phillips and be around other professional athletes would be life-changing. This could potentially get me to the Olympic Games scheduled for the next year. I also knew I had more room to improve my long jump distance after college. This was also coupled with the fact that I could obtain dual citizenship with the country of Honduras.

My mother being born in Honduras granted me the option to professionally compete for her home country instead of the USA. After my initial conversation with Ryan Billian, I began research-ing ways to connect with the Honduras track team. Through this online research, I found out about the Honduran track athlete Gerom Solis. He was still in college at the time, at Iona College in New York. However, I could not find his social media or a way to contact him to ask about competing for Honduras! Weeks later at Penn Relays in Philadelphia, as I had just gotten off the subway train, I saw members of the Iona College track team across the street. I immediately wondered if I would be able to meet Gerom. Eventually, his team came to my side of the street. Then, I saw a name badge that read "Gerom Solis." I introduced myself and told him I was looking for ways to connect with the Honduran team so I could run professionally. He gave me every contact I needed!

The younger me would have chosen to compete for Team USA because it typically has the best track athletes (since the USA has a larger population and better resources than most other countries), and I wanted to go against the best! However, with age came wisdom, and it made more sense to choose the path of least resistance. I would also train with my friend Ryan Billian and other professionals, receive coaching from Dwight Phillips, and shoot for the Olympics within a specific timeframe. With all these available factors, I chose to go for it! I thought of this decision from a third-person point of view. If I had friends with the same opportunities I had, I would tell them to do the same.

I waited until October 2019 to begin professional training because my body needed rest from my last collegiate seasons. I also knew professional seasons spanned for longer than college seasons. I was in Cincinnati, Ohio at the time I made my decision to compete professionally. I reached out to David Payne and asked if he would coach me. David Payne is a Cincinnati native and an Olympic silver medalist. Although he was a hurdler and not a long jumper, he had vast knowledge of the sport and con-nections that would aid me. I also reconnected with Garrett Stoller, who was the first athletic trainer I had in college. I found out that he left Miami University to be in Cincinnati full-time as an entrepreneur with the baseball performance company, Elite SC. I also had my first encounter with chiropractic care, thanks to a recommendation from Rod Mills. He recommended that I see Dr. Greg Pitman since he was the father of Grant Pitman, who also went to Miami with us. From there I had what I thought I needed to succeed, and I ran with it. Pun intended!

After a couple of months of training in Cincinnati, I received some nagging injuries, and I had to deal with freezing weather. I finessed my way into a coaching conference in Orlando, Florida so I could train in warmer weather. I knew it was time for a change. With the help of Ryan Billian, I made the long jump from Cincinnati, Ohio to Atlanta, Georgia to expand my training for the Olympics. This allowed me to be coached by Dwight Phillips alongside former NCAA champions like Zack Bazile and Marquise Goodwin, who is also a former Olympian. With the help of family members, I was able to live in Atlanta while I trained. This move was exciting but not entirely what I expected it to be.

The first couple of weeks, I was just excited to be in the presence of so much greatness! Our training group comprised of athletes from all over the U.S. and other countries such as Nigeria, the United Kingdom, Italy, the British Virgin Islands, Russia, and Jamaica. I learned more about the technical aspects of track by listening to Dwight Phillips and Dr. Marco Belizaire. Sadly, the COVID-19 outbreak in March of 2020 caused everything to shut down right before the outdoor season was set to begin. Therefore, track facilities began to close their gates, forcing my decision to pause training until the pandemic had calmed down. I drove back to my Ohio family since there was talk about state lines being closed. The Olympic Committee then chose to postpone the 2020 Olympic Games until 2021.

After the world gained a slight understanding of the pandemic situation and things in the U.S. began to open back up, I returned to Atlanta in September to continue training. I was excited because it is always fun to reconnect with teammates and get back to the grind! However, for multiple instances in consecutive months we were forced to stop in the middle of practice. Police officials would see us training and say COVID-19 was the reason we could no longer use the facility. This was a contradiction, as exercise and being outside are some of the best ways to strengthen the immune system. It was also disappointing because we were Olympic athletes on the path to achieving our dreams. We hopped around to different facilities around the city, and we even had to change our practice times to avoid police interaction. This was certainly an added stressor.

In November, the weather began to be a stressor as well because contrary to popular belief, IT GETS COLD IN ATLANTA! Thankfully, Coach Dwight established a connection with SPIRE Institute in Geneva, Ohio. They had an indoor track facility and the capacity to house and feed us during a winter training camp. It seemed well overpriced, but many of my friends and family members donated money to help me pay. This situation was not the best, but I had to be grateful and make it work. I needed it to properly prepare for my first international meet and opportunity to represent Honduras. In late December, I would be competing in Costa Rica at the Central American Championships.

At the meet, I did not perform well in the long jump. I was projected to win a gold medal but earned a bronze medal instead by one centimeter. I blamed this performance on being super rusty, and it was my first time implementing my new, longer runway approach. Fortunately, the next day, I was able to redeem myself. Our team—composed of Melique Garcia, Yariel Matute, Gerom Solis, and me—won the 4x100 meter relay and broke the Honduran record! Just like in college, I was the anchor leg who brought it home for us while staring at the clock. Symbolically, Gerom Solis, the same guy who met me in Philadelphia and introduced me to the Honduran connections I needed, would be the person to hand me the baton.

At this moment, I realized how "American" I was. We had just accomplished an amazing feat, but I was not as ecstatic as my teammates due to comparing our time to what I have witnessed in the USA. We would have gotten smoked by a college team. My mother helped me realize how comparison is the thief of joy. Her words helped me to enjoy what we accomplished. As I returned to Atlanta in January to continue training for the outdoor season,

Coach Dwight decided that our training group would go to Miami, Florida in February for a three-week training camp in warmer weather.

Fraternity Benefits and Social Media

In this section, I will share another example of fraternity benefits and using social media wisely. I messaged Brandon Marshall, a retired NFL wide receiver and fellow Kappa man. Brandon is also the CEO of the brand and world-class athletic facility House of Athlete in Weston, Florida. Since Weston was only 30 minutes away from Miami, I knew this would be the perfect opportunity to tour House of Athlete and train at its amazing facility. Most people would be discouraged by their own thoughts and assume that a celebrity would not reply to them. However, I am not one of those people, and whoever reads this should let go of those kinds of thoughts. If you are holding on to fearful thoughts, you are BLOCKING YOUR BLESSINGS! I went to Brandon Marshall's Instagram and saw it had the option to text his phone number. I introduced myself via text and included that we were fraternity brothers. He quickly replied, stating that he would be ecstatic to have me and my teammates come to his facility to train during our trip. After my initial message, my teammates and I were able to speak directly with Brandon Marshall and many of the staff members. Those conversations have now formed lifelong connections that we each benefit from.

Injuries, Competing, and Traveling

In Miami, Florida, there are also plenty of temptations and reasons why it is nicknamed "Vice City." As a heterosexual man, my vice was women, and Miami has a plethora of them from all nationalities! I feel like my distractions played a part in what happened next. On the first Friday of our trip, the day we were prepared to long jump at practice, I strained my groin while sprinting. I analyzed everything that occurred up to this point.

First, I did not get much sleep the night before. My teammates and I were up late playing card games with some women we met. I was also dehydrated because I went against my normal way of operating during training phases. To not be labeled as a wimp, I decided to drink alcohol. But something else was off. I realized that my ankle injury from college had never fully healed, and my feet were weak! This created all sorts of compensation, tightness, and pain throughout my entire body. I attempted to mask these aspects with all types of modalities and solutions that provided comfort.

While still recovering from my injury, my mother informed me that she was planning to visit Honduras in March for her birthday. I knew this would be a great opportunity for multiple reasons besides celebrating with her and my sister. The trip would be my first time visiting Honduras, I would be able to see certain family members, and my mother could be my English to Spanish translator in the areas I lacked. Also, I would get to relax and de-stress while enjoying the beautiful scenery that Honduras has to offer.

People often refer to Honduras as a third-world country, but many parts seem just like the United States. There were shopping malls, grocery stores, and American-based fast-food restaurants. The scenery was amazing at the various beaches, waterfalls, and lakes, plus they were not overcrowded. Something I found interesting and different from the United States was the neighborhoods where mansion-sized houses stood right beside small shacks.

I advise everyone to travel internationally at least once so you can see and experience what truly occurs instead of relying on what others say. This trip with my family was much needed, and with my return to the United States, I knew it was time to refocus on making the Olympics so I could make my family and Honduras proud.

By late April, I had partially recovered enough to compete in track meets as a professional in the U.S. These were some amazing experiences, as I met legends and celebrities like Justin Gatlin, Sha'Carri Richardson, and Chad "Ochocinco" Johnson. At my first meet in San Diego, California, I still managed to jump close to 25 feet after not being able to sprint for 40 days after my injury. I remember a time when 25 feet was my peak, but at this point, I could do it while injured. I can only imagine what I could have long jumped with a healthy and balanced body! Yet, 25 feet was two feet short of what I would need for Olympic qualifications. I competed in more meets in Georgia but still could not hit the Olympic standard.

Shortly after the meet in San Diego, Coach Dwight decided to stop coaching certain athletes for the remainder of the season, including me. He felt like there were too many athletes in the group who began to disrespect him and not take training seriously. I respected his decision and explained how serious my injury was. He and I are still friends today, but this separation allowed me to learn even more about long jumping, as I had to become more self-dependent. I am thankful that I also had fellow long jumpers such as Ryan Billian and Reggie Steele to confide in and receive necessary help from. We each began to have new revelations and ideas about training as professional athletes.

At the end of the season, I had another opportunity to compete in Costa Rica for another year of the Central American Championships. This time, however, my body was in shambles. My groin had not fully healed, and it led to other injuries from overcompensating and not giving my body proper time or resources to recover. The first day of the competition consisted of the 100-meter dash and the 4x100 meter relay. I was unprepared for the 100-meter dash, and I ran my slowest time ever. Then, our relay team did not have the same team members as the prior championships. One of our top sprinters decided to retire due to the lack of financial assistance and professionalism we received from our country. I was still the anchor leg but not able to sprint at my best and get our team a gold medal. The next day, I would compete in the long jump, have a chance to make up for my disappointing performance at the previous championships, and potentially qualify for the Olympics.

I gave it my all and competed against the reigning gold medalist from Costa Rica. Throughout the competition, I continually sat in second place but kept going for first! Eventually, I pushed my body past its limits, and I strained my hamstring on my last jump attempt for the gold. I could not even walk afterward, and I had to be taken to an emergency room in an ambulance. This type of injury ended my season, which meant no Olympics. I thought I would be sad, but I was relieved to finally get some rest. Family and friends who supported me were still proud of me for going on the journey and achieving medals at the Central American Championships. I told my parents I would heal and then aim for the World Championships next season.

Dear Kenny,

If you are considering becoming a professional athlete, be sure to analyze every factor as you will be under pressure emotionally, physically, spiritually, and financially. I spent over $10,000 to recover my body with modalities like chiropractor visits, acupuncture, muscle activation, compression boots, cupping, and more! I spent another $3,000 on coaching, $6,000 on housing, and $5,000 on groceries and restaurants. That may or may not seem like much, but that is drastic when we consider that I paid zero dollars in college.

It took me being a professional athlete and going through these tribulations to appreciate the benefits that colleges provide to athletes by way of coaching, housing, food, physical therapy, and access to facilities.

Sincerely,

Kenny Glenn, Success Coach and Entrepreneur

My Experience in Politics

Once I graduated from college and returned home, multiple people within my school district informed me that two board seats were up for election. They insisted that I would make a perfect school board member. I had no clue what a school board member did or that it would require a campaign. With proper assistance and guidance from good-hearted politicians, I went through the process of receiving donations, creating flyers and posterboards with my name, and speaking with voters in different settings. I even stood on a street corner during school dismal while holding one of my signs so parents could see who I was and eventually vote for me.

I quickly learned that politics is a dirty game and that it reveals the true colors of everyone involved. Individuals to whom I had not spoken with in years donated to my campaign! I became privy to information and stories I had no business knowing, but I suddenly became everyone's best friend. Certain individuals were running in the election who very few community members wanted to see win. My campaign would serve as a buffer to ensure this did not happen.

On election day, I stood outside of my closest polling location and let voters know to choose me on their ballot. My parents and girlfriend also helped with this. When the results were tallied, I had achieved third place in the voting by 300 votes, but I needed to be first or second to earn a seat. I was not upset. I did the best

I could, and I helped to ensure that the individuals who would not progress our district were not voted in.

However, shortly after the election, the acting president of the board resigned! This left an open seat for me to fill! I gladly put in my letter of interest to assure the remaining members that I would like to fill the seat. At the first board meeting, it was up to the members to decide if they would choose me, and they did. It was a sigh of relief to me and everyone who supported or voted for me.

As a board member, I saw how most politicians and people in power positions are way too accustomed to doing things the same way as in the past. The hardest part about serving in a position like this is knowing the truth behind decisions but not being able to share them with anyone outside of executive session meetings. People also began to treat me with much more respect and kindness than before I earned the title of "board member." Teachers and administrators acted as if I had the power to fire them, but that was far from reality. My main responsibilities were to hire and evaluate the performances of the district's superintendent and treasurer. My other duties were to vote on impactful aspects, financial purchases, and expulsion appeal hearings.

This experience also taught me the ins and outs of the school system, such as the finances behind every decision. Those decisions include staff employment and hiring contractors to update facilities or improve our district. The timing of my term allowed me to serve before and during the COVID-19 pandemic, which meant that I was able to attend meetings virtually and temporarily live in Atlanta, Georgia while training for the Olympics. Also, just a few months into my term, I was responsible for hiring a new superintendent. Here I was, at 22 years of age, asking individuals who were born 40+ years before me, why I should choose them to lead our district.

I am extremely grateful for the remarkable things that occurred during my tenure, such as approving the construction of our Early Learning Center (thanks to Superintendents Dr. Reva Cosby & Dr. Valerie Hawkins) and using grant money to bring back school buses for high school students after nearly a 10-year hiatus! I also established relationships with some amazing people who are truly passionate about creating the changes and improvements necessary to benefit the students they serve.

A Global Pandemic

At the time I write this book (2021-2022) we are living in an interesting period. The COVID-19 pandemic has shifted the minds and behaviors of billions across the globe. Technology and virtual reality have rapidly advanced and have been widely adopted by the masses. We no longer must travel outside of our homes to see or meet people. Virtual reality has made some experiences seem so "real" that many are now uncertain of the difference between natural and artificial.

One of the reasons why I turned down my full-time job offer with KPMG in 2019 was that they told me the only way I could switch to a more preferred department was to move to a big city. I asked, "Why? Why is it mandatory for me to move to a big city and pay higher rent to perform a job that requires over 80% travel? Why can't I live in Cincinnati but live out of my suitcase and join calls when and where I am needed?" It was mind-boggling to them back then, but now almost everyone in their company has the ability to work from home and contribute virtually. Dr. Baker & Associates and other innovative companies were already using communication platforms like Zoom long before it became an "overnight" phenomenon. There was a time when consultants would have to travel by train, boat, or plane to see and speak with their clients. But with today's technological advancements, businesses can serve their clients from anywhere with an internet connection.

This pandemic has also altered the way we conduct schooling, work, and family life. You are no longer tied to a physical location to complete certain tasks. Although it should not have been in the first place, your definition of success is no longer confined to a certain job, title, salary, or a specific city. Sadly, many people needed this pandemic to pause their fast-paced lifestyles and reevaluate what was truly important. It also reminded us that we are free to choose and create our optimal lives and career paths. These things may seem obvious, but the obvious should never be overlooked.

Dear Kenny,

I write these words as a reminder that no matter what occurs in the outside world, you will always have the power and resources to be fruitful and live abundantly. You will accomplish your definition of success by thinking creatively, mastering the necessary skills, and keeping a positive attitude! Doing these things will help you find what you love and eventually make money in your sleep!

But how? Take heed to these words: "My passion will lead me to my purpose."

Sincerely,

Kenny Glenn, Success Coach and Entrepreneur

CHAPTER 15

Kenny's Lifestyle Changes

In this chapter, I get more personal as I discuss recent revelations in my life. After 17 years of school, I jumped into "the real world" and tried to treat life like a continuation of school. Yet, my versions of school did not prepare me for things like dealing with depression or truly being in charge of where I spent my time. School taught and rewarded me for being good at or involved with everything. In my post-grad life, I quickly learned the meaning of the phrase "less is more." I tried to be Superman by grabbing every title, joining all types of organizations, and packing my days with phone calls and meetings. This led to mental, physical, and emotional burnout.

Looking back, it is funny how often my parents and romantic partners would tell me to "sit down" as a way of telling me to get some rest. Hearing those words felt like an insult because of how I was programmed to be impulsive and always GRIND, GRIND, GRIND! Quotes and sayings like "If you're not working, your competition is!" or "All gas, no brakes" began to devour me. As a mental analogy, "All gas, no brakes" makes sense when you are on a racetrack, but not when you are driving from New York to

California. Rest and breaks (pun intended) are necessary when seeking to achieve big goals.

During and after my professional track season, I learned the benefits of rest and how opposites are equally important. To use athletics as an example, rest and recovery are JUST AS important as exercising. We do not always have to be doing some type of mental or physical activity related to our sport. Sometimes, it is beneficial to literally DO NOTHING.

Dear Kenny,

Regardless of how digital the world becomes or how much it pushes you to work nonstop, I want you to log off and get into nature! We were not created to be working or in meetings all day long. Especially not staring at screens with artificial light. No more "GRIND, GRIND, GRIND!" I would rather work four hours at 100% effort, than work eight hours at 50% effort. I know you do not want to be called "lazy," but working efficiently is better than wasting time and effort.

Take a walk in the park. Take a nap. Smile. Pick up a book. Take the necessary time to recharge away from technology. Meditate, sit with your thoughts, and express gratitude. Give your brain and your body a break.

Sincerely,

Kenny Glenn, Success Coach and Entrepreneur

Still Running Track?

After accumulating so many serious injuries, I began doing hours of anatomy research to learn how the body is truly supposed to function. It became clear how in our society, we have been rewarded for imbalance. If you look at models in fitness magazines, you will notice their chests, biceps, abs, quads, glutes, and calves... BUT WHAT ABOUT THE OPPOSING MUSCLES!? They are less prominent but equally important! Something as simple as walking backward has amazing healing effects on the body because of the activation of the antagonistic muscles we use when walking forward. That is a simple yet mind-boggling fact! This activity is what makes basketball and soccer more demanding than other sports. You must constantly move your body in all directions: forward, backward, and side to side. Most humans and most track athletes only move their bodies straight ahead. Moving your body in one direction too much in comparison to other directions will create the very thing that causes all pain, injury, and dis-ease: IMBALANCE.

For this truth, I also have Sumair Bhasin (the Unstoppable Baller), Derek Williams (MR1NF1N1TY), Ben Patrick (KneesOverToesGuy), and Stefan Duvivier (Mind Your Movement) to thank for their assistance, confirmation, and passion in spreading this information to the masses. We are living in a time when preventable surgeries and injuries are at an all-time high and are continuing to increase. I respect the doctors and trainers who do the right thing by providing optimal solutions to the best of their knowledge. But I do not respect the crooked system that continues to profit by promoting unnecessary surgeries, harmful injections, and pain medications. These avoidable realities cause massive debt, depression, and destruction to the body.

Dear Kenny,

Everything you need you were already born with, and your body can heal itself when given the correct information. Information comes from food, environment, and life education.

Today, more than ever, we have limitless information at our fingertips. Study the athletes who perform amazing feats yet have minimal injuries.

They have not only trained and strengthened the popular muscle groups but also the opposing and less popular muscle groups such as the back, triceps, hamstrings, hip flexors, tibialis, feet, and ankles. They understand that our chances of injury increase when we only strengthen the muscles we can see but not the tendons and ligaments they are attached to.

Sincerely,

Kenny Glenn, Success Coach and Entrepreneur

I originally planned to continue training as a professional track athlete, but I knew multiple changes would be necessary. I thought about moving to California or Florida to train with coaches who better aligned with my new knowledge of the sport. But as the weeks got closer to when I planned to start training, I took the necessary time to reflect. I asked myself if track was something I seriously wanted to continue. Did I want to overly stress my mind, body, and relationships for more track success? The answer I came up with was… "NOPE."

Although I did not qualify for the 2020 Olympics, I still have opportunities to compete in more Olympic Games in track and field in the future. Yet, I am choosing not to, and I have no regrets! Track gave me everything I needed from it and more! It helped pay for college, allowed me to create joy while earning accolades, and meet so many amazing people from around the world with whom I have created lifelong relationships. I realized that I was running professional track mainly for external factors like company sponsorships, fame, spotlight, and titles. These reasons outweighed internal factors such as feelings of enjoyment, achievement, and belonging. We live in a world where sometimes you must do what you have to do. However, you should eventually reach a point where you start to do what you truly love and want to do.

In terms of sport, my true love is still basketball, and I plan to leverage my dual citizenship and athleticism to play for Honduras in some capacity. Even if I never play in Honduras, basketball is a sport I play for fun at gyms and tournaments in every city I visit. This is my choice, and I am happy with it, whether others agree or not. Some people may think I should just stick to track like people thought Kanye West should just stick to producing beats. Kanye continued to prove that he could rap with the best and then sold quadruple platinum rap albums! What if he had just listened to those who doubted him and did not see the gift that he and his mother saw? Everything has a time and place, and no one should place a limit on their self-belief.

My self-belief has gotten to the point where people I interact with believe I am going to do whatever I say and put my mind to because I have consistently proven it. Strangers even believe me based on my passion! Sometimes I might sound crazy, but I think crazy is necessary. The Wright Brothers had to be somewhat crazy and delusional to think they could create airplanes! But they successfully created airplanes after learning from their "thousands" of failed attempts. You may even be reading this book while riding in an airplane.

The Realities of Entrepreneurship

The stress of searching for new clients or constantly being rejected took a toll on my mental health, my financial health, and my romantic relationship. Although I was learning at a rapid pace, and helping create real change, I was stuck in the rat race of chasing money. I also was responsible for lots of financial model-ing and accounting information reviews for clients. My passion for helping businesses has not faded, but the way I do it has changed. One day, I wrote a note to myself explaining how I truly hated accounting, and I entitled it "My Passion." It reads: "I hate accounting. I am a creative problem solver who understands the importance of finances. Although I have my Master's in Accounting, it is not where my passion lives or thrives."

Looking back on Buku Ibraheem's quote, "Turn your passion into a paycheck," I am now living that lifestyle, and my younger self would be proud of me! I previously tried to box myself into accounting because it married together numbers and people, it was highly respectable, and I knew that accountants would always be needed. But I was limiting myself and my creative ability! Technically, everything deals with numbers, and unless you are in a back office, in isolation, you will interact with people. As an educational consultant and public speaker, I help students and business owners strategically simplify their lives to achieve their goals. My greatest passion is helping people realize their potential and leading them in the best direction to achieve their dreams. It brings internal satisfaction when I mentor and inspire students and graduates between the ages of 12 and 24.

Another aspect of entrepreneurship is the high rate of failure mainly due to lack of funds, ineffective business models, inability to sell, or inadequate teams. I tried to go into business with a close friend, and in hindsight, it was a terrible idea! There was a great opportunity to easily earn over six figures, but I did not properly vet my friend's potential to be a business owner. They had low business acumen on top of being financially illiterate and immature. My advice here is to be exceedingly cautious about the people you choose to do business with before you lose valuable time, money, and energy. Set protocols, guidelines, and payback schedules if you loan out start-up capital.

Educational Passion

My board term ended after two years instead of four because I took over the remaining time of the previous board member who resigned. I noticed the problems within the school system before, during, and after my time as a board member. School districts are facing problems that are not singular or unique. Instead, most school districts throughout the country are dealing with the same problems. I find it interesting how the same aspects that Dr. Jawanza Kunjufu outlined during multiple speeches about education in 1988, are still relevant today. I invite you to watch some of his videos on YouTube.

During my school board tenure, I met and worked with some amazing people as we aimed to push the district forward on all fronts. However, being a board member did limit me in some capacities. I realized the best way to make a difference was to grow my original passion of pouring into students and graduates. The passion I am referring to is what I am choosing to do now, which is creating and providing real solutions and role models for students and graduates to benefit from. Contrary to popular belief, students and graduates listen to advice. It just depends on who the advice comes from. Often, there is a misalignment when teachers and administrators do not have similar backgrounds as the students or do not look like them. It is time to create, find, and implement innovative solutions and organizations like the He Is Me Institute and Educ8theWORLD.

Here are some of the ideas I wrote before joining the school board. These ideas remain useful and resonate with every school in America, especially those with predominantly Black student populations.

1. Increase the number of opportunities and resources available to students before and after graduation (such as internships, educational summer camps, and after-school programs) and help students open their minds to taking advantage of them.

2. Gain strategic partnerships with mentor groups, local businesses, banks, and colleges to improve financial literacy. Include students at all grade levels and their parents.

3. Partner with HBCUs and organizations that focus on solutions to increase the number & retention of Black teachers.

During my board tenure, civil unrest in America was widespread after the murder of George Floyd by Minneapolis police. Floyd's murder sent the entire nation into a frenzy, especially in places with high percentages of Black Americans. I was asked to write a letter since I was a Black man and a community figure who would attract listeners. I chose not to publicly release the letter when I originally wrote it because some felt uneasy with my choice of words. I also did not want to personally deal with the potential backlash on social media because I would not have cared to reply. Here is an excerpt from that letter:

It is okay for students to feel every emotion under the sun about the constant and consistent oppression that Black Americans face. However, there are multiple ways and strategies to go about creating that needed change.

A Call to Action: Students need to see and interact with those who look like them and share similar backgrounds. Our students need positive Black role models. I challenge each person who uses their words, time, and energy to complain about our students to shift that energy to help them and their various situations. We need new partnerships with Black business owners, company executives, and role models that our students can see, communicate with, and be mentored by. Our school district needs to strengthen our connection with Black alumni as well. Even if a graduate was not the best student during their high school career, their story, their pitfalls, and their achievements after high school are still worth being shared with our students. These will show students what they can aspire to become with the necessary steps but also what to avoid.

While in high school, one of my Black assistant principals would get on the school intercom and say every day, "BE THE CHANGE YOU WANT TO SEE IN

THE WORLD." That is now the task and mindset that we should all have to put an end to racism and oppression by enacting change to the current unjust system and powers that be.

I write this message as a Black Man in America, a son, a brother, a mentor, a Mt. Healthy graduate, a Mt. Healthy School Board Member, and a Mt. Healthy community member.

Nutritional Change

Nutrition is an extremely touchy subject because people have become addicted to certain unhealthy foods with an unwillingness to change. My advice is to do your own research and gather information from multiple sources. Then, apply what you find by trying and eliminating certain foods to find what is best for you. What sparked me to change the food I ate was acne flare-ups and a decrease in athletic capability due to soreness & slow recovery. I tried all types of acne treatments for my face and many modalities for my body, but nothing worked until I changed what I ate. A major plus is getting more natural sunlight to get sufficient levels of Vitamin D along with the positive hormones of serotonin and dopamine.

To further emphasize the point of nutrition and how environment plays a role, I will use a neighborhood example. Neighborhoods with residents who have low income and low credit scores are still riddled with businesses that do not serve their best interests. As an example of how your external environment affects your health and nutritional intake, I will use a neighborhood in Cincinnati, Ohio.

One day while pumping gas, I took time to scan the surrounding businesses. I have driven through this neighborhood thousands of times but never noticed just how bad it was. There is a check-cashing place next to a liquor store, a vape shop, and five cheap fast-food restaurants. None of these things promote health, wealth, or wellness! Nor are they for the betterment of our minds, bodies, or neighborhoods! There is a reason they call places like these "the trap!" They trap people into negativity and the perception that such a way of living is normal.

As a Black American, I adopted the standard eating habits that were thrown to my ancestors during Trans-Atlantic slavery. Just because something tastes good does not mean it is good for you or that you should eat it. My grandfather died from high blood pressure and diabetes because of what he ate. It was a consistent diet of pork in all forms, heavily fried and salted foods, starchy food, and dairy products. As a child, I was ignorant of the harmful effects of these foods, and I did not have much of a say in what my parents cooked.

By now choosing to reject these old eating habits and learning what I should be eating to live more healthily, I am reversing disease and aging. The decreased inflammation has helped my mind, body, and soul, as they are all connected. Now, I know that when it comes to nutritional marketing, we have been hoodwinked.

My nutritional intake has transitioned to more natural alkaline fruits and foods, which were taught by Alfredo Bowman, more famously known as Dr. Sebi. Something I do not believe in is co-incidences. It is no coincidence that Dr. Sebi and my mother were both born in Honduras. I became aware of Dr. Sebi thanks to his descendants speaking of the healing powers of certain foods and herbs like sea moss and sarsaparilla. My knowledge base expounded even more as I read the book *My Journey with Dr. Sebi*, which was written by his trusted friend Abelardo Guerrero Jr. I thank my cousin Anthony Johnson for allowing me to borrow the book to absorb the information and apply it to my life.

Before making my nutritional transformation, I consumed heavy amounts of animals and high starch sources of protein because this is what I and most American athletes have been sold that we need for muscle growth, strength, and recovery. In my first semester of college, I mostly ate barbeque chicken wings, French fries, pizza, chocolate whole milk, and large bags of candy. My eating habits did not change until women from the track team advised me to eat more healthily because it would help with performance. I started to eat more fruit, salads, and baked foods for my caloric intake.

I must note that I am an extremist. This means that I can cut things or habits off in an instant. I have unconsciously been on this journey since the age of 12, as this is when I decided to no longer drink soda because of the massive amounts of white sugar in it. Next, at the age of 18, I decided to give up drinking cow milk, as one of my teammates explained to me how cow milk was not created for human consumption. It was overwhelming to me how simple but true her statement was, but also how delicious other kinds of milk (almond, coconut, and hemp) were.

Next, I decided to give up pork after learning the harmful effects of consuming it. I fully understand there was a time when my ancestors were fed pork and had to make the best of it. However, those times are over! Today, we only cling to it because of traditional mental shackles, marketing, easy availability, and seasoning. But these traditional diets (keyword "die") are failing us! The time is now to create new traditions, rather than continue to follow those that continually fail us. This includes, but is not limited to, traditional food choices, the traditional school system, the traditional ways of fitness and health, and the traditional disciplinary and judicial system.

You may be wondering what foods I eat since I have cut out what is heavily marketed. I eat the foods I need to survive and thrive. The foods the Creator of this universe made for me to eat. Foods that line up with my ancestral traits and cause minimal to no harm to my body. These foods give me energy and electrify my mind, body, and soul. I eat food for information, not inflammation. For me, no longer consuming animals eliminated severe inflammation and the unhealthy imbalance of hormones. It also caused me to be less angry and more loving. A portion of the meals and smoothies I prepare stem from the food list that Dr. Sebi outlined. You can check out if you want.

My advice about food is to "keep it simple." Be conscious about what you put into your body because you only get one. Your body is a temple and the tool to help you experience life to the fullest. Stay away from processed foods, foods with added sugar and salt, and harmful ingredients you cannot pronounce. All those chemicals will negatively affect your taste buds and body because they create unhealthy addictions.

Dear Kenny,

Whatever you choose to eat, ask yourself, "Is there a healthier option?" This will lead you down a rabbit hole of learning what is best for your body and what you eventually will prefer. Read food labels and eat foods with minimal ingredients. You are responsible for what goes inside of your body.

Sincerely,

Kenny Glenn, Success Coach and Entrepreneur

Monk Mode

Part of my lifestyle change outside of nutrition was a new external look. To represent my internal changes, without telling a single person, I got my head shaved completely BALD! Before this time, I had a full head of hair, but in my soul, I knew it was time for a change. A literal fresh start! Out with the old, in with the new! It was a symbol of me letting go of my previous self and embracing the new me with more confidence and freedom than ever before. Here is a fitting quote from Robin Sharma's book

The 5 AM Club: "The life of the caterpillar must end for the glory of the butterfly to shine. The old 'you' must die before the best 'you' can be born."

My hair began thinning in certain areas, and it made me feel insecure. The thinning was certainly due to genetics, but it was also due to the typical American diet and my high stress levels. I could have hidden it with Black Ice, low haircuts, or artificial chemicals like Minoxidil. But these options require time, energy, and money that could be placed into other matters I deemed more important. At the end of the day, I want to be true to myself. I may fool everyone else but not me. I continuously saw the thinning, and the time came to try something new. The factor that shined brightest (besides my extra shiny scalp) with my decision to shave my head was fearlessness.

Most men fear going bald as much as they fear public speaking or not following the crowd. Thankfully, I no longer fear these things! I embrace doing empowering tasks because I know the infinite power inside of me. The previous version of me was afraid of all these things, but NOT ANYMORE! I refuse to live as a victim or allow others' thoughts of me to control me. In the greatest movie of all time, *The Matrix*, when Neo woke up after taking the red pill, he did not have a single hair on his body. He was a new man who had to be rebuilt.

While bald, I felt the energy and wisdom of famous people I admire, such as Kobe Bryant. Plus, all my favorite hairstyles involved some sort of baldness. I was bald for three months before I decided to regrow my hair into an afro. I got tired of shaving my head every day since it would grow back so quickly. An afro and a bald head both represent freedom for me, but an afro requires much less maintenance. Since making the nutritional change and using more natural hair products, my hair now grows thicker in the places where it had begun thinning before I shaved all of it.

Conclusion

Thank you for taking the time to read this book. Now, you should understand the difference between school and education. Hopefully, I have shifted your paradigm while also inspiring you to create and pursue your personal definition of success. I define success as being able to freely do what makes me happy while inspiring others. There are still a few more words of advice I would like to share with you.

It is my strong opinion that everyone should write a book. Many people, and maybe even you, will reject this idea and say to themselves, "I can't write a book." My response is: "YOU CAN'T !?" What about the thousands of text messages you have typed and sent, the captions you have written for social media posts, the tweets you have tweeted, your journal entries, and the many conversations you have had? That probably amounts to at least three books! Reflect on your experiences and the valuable lessons you have learned. Then, teach those lessons to others. This is the infinite cycle of life and a key to how we help create a more loving world. How deep are you willing to go? How long are you willing to endure?

Writing is highly therapeutic, and it allows you to reflect on your life and past decisions. This book is a literal culmination of thoughts, poems, and experiences I have typed into my iPhone notes since 2014. That is eight years' worth of knowledge and information. If I had not written this book, where would that information have been used? Some of it would live with the people to whom I told certain stories. However, Dr. Eric Thomas states,

"People forget. Paper does not." This book will live on forever. My great-great-grandchildren will be able to read this and learn about the life experiences of their ancestor. Some authors and artists are no longer here physically, but they will live on through the books and music they created. Luther Vandross passed away in 2005, but his music is still played by millions every day. Napoleon Hill passed away in 1970, but *Think & Grow Rich* is still one of the greatest books written, and people buy it by the thousands every year. I hope that both of their families are still receiving compensation for what they created for others to enjoy and learn from forever!

I now live a passion-filled and purposeful life by inspiring students and graduates. I help them realize their power to be and become who and whatever they want. By doing so, they can have anything they want. You will forever be a student. It does not matter when you graduate or where you graduate from, even if it is only kindergarten. You may not be a student at a specific institution, but you are always learning from the school, the game, and the experience we call life. Throughout my life journey, I have been searching to connect myself to where I belong. I am like Hercules in the eponymous animated Disney movie, as he knew there was something great inside of him that needed to be unleashed. I am also similar to the protagonist Santiago in *The Alchemist* by Paulo Coelho. I always had everything I needed and wanted around me and inside of me, but I had to embark on different journeys to even realize it.

Take the time to sit back and observe the good and the bad around you, the light and the darkness. Where there is bad or darkness, you can be the light or the solution for good. Where there is good, you can learn from it and eventually contribute to making it even better. Too often we neglect or become blinded by the light that is near us. We are ungrateful or unappreciative of the benefits that certain people or things bring until outsiders see the benefit or the benefit is taken away. This is true with relationships, schools, and businesses. Do not only look for solutions to your problems in faraway places, but also use and appreciate what you have inside of you and close to you. Be grateful for everything in your environment and take advantage of the gems in your life.

It is my advice for you to be unafraid in questioning those around you, including teachers, mentors, coaches, friends, so-called experts, and whoever you learn from. I offer you one more quote on this matter from Robert Diggs aka RZA of the hip-hop group Wu-Tang Clan. Featured in Remedy's song entitled "Education," RZA states, **"I stood up like a man. Then, I questioned the teacher."**

I would like to leave you with a list of tips to aid in your success.

Qualities That Will Take Anyone Far in Life:

1. Listening
2. Patience
3. Self-control
4. Discipline
5. Continuous growth in knowledge, wisdom, and understanding

Everyday Habits for Success

- Consistently getting 0.0001% better at something
- Getting off your phone before bed
- Rising out of bed earlier than most
- Meditation
- Metacognition

- Staying hydrated with seeded fruits and water
- Writing in your gratitude journal
- Writing down your goals
- Visualization
- Deep breathing

Helpful Books I Have Read

- *Question Everything: Advice for Students & Graduates* by Kenny Glenn **(RE-READ THIS BOOK)**
- *The Alchemist* by Paulo Coelho
- *The One Thing* by Gary W. Keller and Jay Papasan
- *The Four Agreements: A Practical Guide to Personal Freedom* by Don Miguel Ruiz
- *Atomic Habits: An Easy & Proven Way to Build Good Habits & Break Bad Ones* by James Clear
- *Relentless: From Good to Great to Unstoppable* by Tim Grover
- *Lone Wolf Mentality: A Millennial Mindset* by Benjamin Phillips III
- *The Mamba Mentality: How I Play* by Kobe Bryant
- *Champion's Mind: How Great Athletes Think, Train, and Thrive* by Jim Afremow, PhD
- *No Debt Zone: Your 9 Step Guide to a Debt Free Life* by Ashley Brewster
- *God Made You Perfect: A Believer's Guide to Perfection* by Dr. J.C. Baker
- *Voice of The Ancestors: Volume 1* by Chase McGhee
- *Rich Dad Poor Dad: What the Rich Teach Their Kids About Money That the Poor and Middle Class Do Not* by Robert Kiyosaki

- *The Way of The Superior Man* by David Deida
- *Disrupting Fitness: Four Paradigm Shifts to Live an Infinity Lifestyle* by Derek Williams
- *The Laws of Human Nature* by Robert Greene
- *How to Win Friends and Influence People* by Dale Carnegie
- *The 4-Hour Body: An Uncommon Guide to Rapid Fat-Loss, Incredible Sex, and Becoming Superhuman* by Tim Grover
- *Think & Grow Rich* by Napoleon Hill
- *The Money Myths* by Jullien Gordon
- *The Will to Win: 7 Laws to Winning* by Dwight Phillips
- *Paradigm Keys: Solution-Based Mind Reprogramming* by 19 Keys
- *The 5 AM Club* by Robin Sharma
- *Why Didn't They Teach Me This in School? 99 Personal Money Management Principles to Live By* (Cary Siegel)
- *Outliers: The Story of Success* by Malcolm Gladwell

Quick Advice

- Let go of the victim mentality. You are a victor!
- Be a creator! You create your reality.
- Be inquisitive. Be intentional with your actions. Take initiative.
- Be grateful for where you are and ambitious about where you are going.
- You do not have to follow the crowd. Make your own path.
- It is okay to say "No" to things you do not want to do.
- What you think about yourself is far more important than what others think.
- There is no such thing as cocky. There is only confidence, doubt, delusion, and deceit.

- You never know who is watching or who you are inspiring on your journey.
- Define yourself.
- Question the words and phrases that people use.
- Constantly seek to become the best version of yourself.
- Learn from the past, live in the present, and plan for the future.
- Be patient, but do not procrastinate. Do not rush. Enjoy the journey.
- Write about your life and the lessons you have learned.
- Increase your emotional intelligence so you can stop reacting and start responding. When you react, it is based on emotion. When you respond, it is based on logic.
- Accept responsibility and stop looking for things or people to blame.
- It may not be your fault that something happened to you, but it is your responsibility to push through it or adapt.
- We are a combination of everyone we have come into some type of contact with.
- Travel! Experience new places, new people, new thoughts, and new ideas. Then, compare what you have heard to what you have seen.
- **Make your younger self proud! Be the person you needed. Write the book you needed to read. Sing the song you needed to hear. Create the tool you needed to use.**
- Always remember: **QUESTION EVERYTHING!**

ABOUT THE AUTHOR

Kenneth Jamall Glenn, better known as Kenny Glenn, is the Founder of Maximo Impact LLC, an Educational Consultant, and a Motivational Speaker. Widely recognized for his passion and ability to inspire others, Kenny is on the forefront of a movement that promotes self-education and self-mastery. In doing so, students and graduates will be equipped to learn the necessary skills to achieve their personal definition of success.

Kenny Glenn was raised in Hampton, Virginia, and Cincinnati, Ohio. Mr. Glenn excelled as an All-State Track Athlete in high school, then went on to set collegiate records at Miami University (Ohio), as well as national records for the country of Honduras. He graduated from Miami University with his Master's and Bachelor's Degrees in Accounting from the prestigious Farmer School of Business. Mr. Glenn previously served as a Board Member for the Mt. Healthy City Schools District, which is the same school district where he graduated middle and high school. Here is where he recognized the greatness waiting to be discovered, and the problems that need to be solved in the school and education system.

Kenny has worked in various roles, such as being a Program Associate with the Leading Men Fellowship in Cincinnati. This group is sponsored by The Literacy Lab, which aims to increase the literacy of young students of color. Also included in the company's goal is increasing the number of male teachers of color.

Kenny genuinely enjoys the process of learning, growing, and venturing new paths. His upbringing instilled the powerful desire to help others, which he now uses to creatively assist and inspire individuals, schools, and businesses to realize their limitless potential and achieve their goals.

Kenny is available to speak to your school, church, organization, or event panel. For more information, please visit www.kgmaximo.com or email info@kgmaximo.com